A RENAISSANCE

OF OUR OWN

A RENAISSANCE OF OUR OWN

"A bold tale of imagination, bravery, and radical action in the face of injustice . . . Through an account of [Rachel E.] Cargle's own complicated life journey, she provides a framework for our own acts of courage as brutality threatens to strip us of humanity."
—*Elle*

"Activist and lecturer Cargle shares how she transformed her life by reimagining herself in terms of faith, relationships, feminism, education, work, and rest. . . . For readers who want to reimagine their role in fighting injustice, she shares her knowledge, empathy, and action (KEA) framework, an effective way to communicate and form diverse allyships. Cargle's self-help memoir is highly recommended for DEI and LGTBQ+ collections and women of all ages who want to renew and rethink their purpose in life."
—*Booklist* (starred review)

"A vulnerable look at one activist's long journey of deconstruction, healing, and reimagining of the toxic societal structure meant to oppress marginalized identities . . . Cargle opens the door into a possibility-rich world of acceptance, accountability, and allyship."
—*Kirkus Reviews*

"I loved and admired this book as much as I have always loved and admired its author. Rachel Cargle is that rare sort of phoenix who rises from the ashes of her life not only reborn on the personal level but also fully ready to change the world. She is a leader of extraordinary power and influence. With each of her reinventions, she has liberated not only herself but numberless others as well. *A Renaissance of Our Own* is an elegant, thoughtful, vulnerable, and inspiring memoir. May this book land in a million hands, all over the world."
—Elizabeth Gilbert, #1 *New York Times* bestselling author of *Big Magic*

"A profoundly moving and powerful story of how one woman transformed both herself and her community while giving us the tools to do the same . . . Rachel Cargle shows that the closer we get to our own true light, the brighter we may shine for the world. You will celebrate, you will mourn, but ultimately you will leave these pages changed for the better."

—Gabrielle Union, *New York Times* bestselling author of *We're Going to Need More Wine*

"Magical, shape-shifting . . . Cargle recounts how she spun silk out of the threadbare yarns of patriarchy and white supremacy while reminding readers that such alchemy is possible. Such wonder is inevitable if we give ourselves permission to reimagine our existences and re-create ourselves in our own divine image."

—Sonya Renee Taylor, *New York Times* bestselling author of *The Body Is Not an Apology*

"Rachel Cargle has given us the gift of an interactive memoir that allows readers to expand into our own renaissance while witnessing hers. She is visionary, revolutionary, unapologetic, and deeply self-loving, reclaiming herself from conditioning that tried to shrink her. In telling her story, Cargle makes more room for each of us."

—adrienne maree brown, *New York Times* bestselling author of *Pleasure Activism: The Politics of Feeling Good*

"What a beautiful offering and gentle invitation Rachel Cargle has extended with *A Renaissance of Our Own*. I felt the pull to really slow down and sit with both her stories and my own. This book is not meant to be simply consumed but explored."

—Joy Harden Bradford, PhD, author of *Sisterhood Heals*

A
RENAISSANCE
OF OUR OWN

A MEMOIR & MANIFESTO
ON REIMAGINING

RACHEL E. CARGLE

BALLANTINE BOOKS

NEW YORK

2024 Ballantine Books Trade Paperback Edition

Published in the United States by Ballantine Books, an imprint of
Random House, a division of Penguin Random House LLC, New York.

BALLANTINE is a registered trademark and the colophon
is a trademark of Penguin Random House LLC.

Originally published in hardcover in the United States
by Ballantine Books, an imprint of Random House,
a division of Penguin Random House LLC, in 2023.

LIBRARY OF CONGRESS CATALOGING-IN-PUBLICATION DATA
NAMES: Cargle, Rachel Elizabeth, author.
TITLE: A renaissance of our own: a memoir & manifesto
on reimagining / Rachel Elizabeth Cargle.
DESCRIPTION: First edition. | New York: Ballantine Books, 2023
IDENTIFIERS: LCCN 2022047562 (print) | LCCN 2022047563 (ebook) |
ISBN 9780593134740 (trade paperback) | ISBN 9780593134757 (ebook)
SUBJECTS: LCSH: Cargle, Rachel Elizabeth. | Anti-racism. |
United States—Race relations.
CLASSIFICATION: LCC HT1563 .C37 2023 (print) |
LCC HT1563 (ebook) | DDC 305.8—dc23/eng/20221201
LC record available at https://lccn.loc.gov/2022047562

Printed in the United States of America on acid-free paper

randomhousebooks.com

2 4 6 8 9 7 5 3 1

Book design by Barbara M. Bachman

For Mom:
Thank you for seeding my curiosity
and growing my courage.

CONTENTS

. . .

MANIFESTO

...

I AM WHO I SAY I AM. I SHAPE MY EXISTENCE WITH CURIOSITY and intention. I honor the spectrum of experiences I have had and will continue to have in this lifetime. Each experience adds to my understanding of the type of woman I decide to be.

My highest values of **ease**, **abundance**, and **opportunity** give me guidance and recalibration toward my truth. They strengthen my "yes" and fortify my "no." I walk confidently with the understanding that my choices are aligned.

My place in the world is sacred. No one knows me better than I know me. I honor and celebrate the ways my chosen self unfolds as I learn, grow, and shift. My beliefs are rooted in my trust that **my current self**, **younger self**, and **older self** are all partners on my path to well-being.

I surround myself with people who affirm **safety**, **kindness**, and **joy**. I maintain boundaries that remind me and others of my needs and my desire to be well. I show up with my very best as a **daughter**, **lover**, **auntie**, **neighbor**, and **friend**.

I hold tight to my belief in **revolution**. Justice is not a passive pursuit but one braided into every way I show up in the world. I name my privileges—**being educated**, **financially secure**, **neuro-typical**, **able-bodied**, and **cisgendered**—and I use them as platforms to fight for the well-being of others.

It is an honor to learn my way through this lifetime. I commit myself to my curiosity and interests. Gaining new and deeper knowledge not only of myself but also of my unique interests, like **art** and **the history of Black feminism,** is always a worthy use of my time.

I have found my work in the world to be rooted in using **my genius as an activist, writer, entrepreneur**, and **philanthropic innovator**. I do my work in a way that aligns with my values and desires.

Rest is a right I hold as a human being. Knowing that my best self is my highest service, I tend generously to my rest and healing—mind, body, and soul. I give myself permission to **let go of perfectionism** and **invest energy into simply being inspired by "the living."**

AUTHOR'S NOTE

...

Dear Reader,

My entire life is a testament to reimagining. What was given to me when I was a child was a life defined by limitations and rules. What was expected *of* me, what was offered *to* me, was barely enough to fit in the palm of my hand.

I was raised by a single mother with a physical disability. We lived in government subsidized housing and depended on welfare. By the time I was in middle school, both my older sisters were battling drug addiction, and my mother had become the primary caregiver for their children. As you can imagine, expectations for *my* own future were dismal.

While I did not have a name for this feeling at the time—I think we would call it ambition—I craved a different life from the one I had been born into. So, I began to reimagine something more for myself. Each step I took away from where I started and toward my vision of a different life led me closer to the place where I am now.

Today, I am a public academic and the CEO of a successful seven-figure business founded in social good—a business

I manifested from a dream I refused to ignore. But it's not where I started. I was once an unhappily married woman living in a small town, trying to convince herself that the voice she was hearing inside her was of value. Luckily, I listened to that voice, and the work I do now is rooted in knowledge sharing and advocating for the rights of Black women and other marginalized groups. I have an online community of nearly two million people from all over the world who have found value in my voice and leadership. And most important, I live a life surrounded by those I love, who love me back and who provide nourishment and goodness to my soul. It's a life that, for a long time, I had only imagined. But then I unearthed the tools to bring this reimagining to life.

And so, as it often happens when we experience life-changing breakthroughs, we want to share them with others. Moments that offer an exciting new lens through which we can view the world can push us to evangelize, to insist that others also consider this new way of living. Perhaps, for you, that breakthrough was a college course that gave you a new framework for considering your place in society. Maybe it was a conversation with your grandmother that uncovered a family truth, shifting what you understood about your lineage and yourself. Or, perhaps, as for me, it was, after years of trying, testing, and pushing back against what was *supposed* to be, discovering the beauty of what *could* be when we give ourselves permission to sample a version of life on the other side of impossible. These realizations, these moments, these experiences, will often both break and fortify us, and the result is that we are never the same. We are reoriented in the world, invited to take the brave step to reimagine.

As you'll read in these pages, I have had several such moments throughout my life—some subtle, some earth-shattering. Each demanded that I reconsider what I understood about both myself and the world around me.

It started when I was a young girl and I began to question what was being taught in the Church. Moving into my teen years, I started to wonder what life might look like outside the cycle of struggle and survival my family was trapped in. As an adult, I questioned the "shoulds" that society often places upon women around relationships, careers, and child-bearing. As an activist, I confronted the whitewashed feminist movement I'd originally been steeped in.

Confronting the ideas and ways of being we find comforting or familiar is no small task. It takes courage and vulnerability to look around at the world we are living in and say, *I want something different.* To some, our reimagining the world might feel like a threat, an invalidation of their truths. To ourselves, this reimagining might feel like a betrayal of a truth we previously were committed to. To the world, our reimagining might seem like a risky, even dangerous, act, since maintaining the status quo is considered both honorable and respectable.

I stand as living proof that a life reimagined is possible—necessary, even—for any person willing to do the work, willing to make peace with the unknown and believe whole-heartedly that they are worth the effort.

This reimagining has been a permission slip allowing me

to explore my fullest potential and most authentic self. My hope is that it becomes a permission slip for you as well— and that, together, as a community, we continue to push past any limit that threatens our freedoms. The more we approach our existence in this way, the stronger our reimagining muscle becomes and the more powerful the reimagining.

> I'll see you on the other side,
> Love, Rachel

A RENAISSANCE
OF OUR OWN

A JOURNEY TO REIMAGINING

...

THERE ARE POINTS IN TIME THAT CAN DIVIDE OUR lives into a "before" and an "after." A moment when a line of demarcation is drawn, after which the lens through which you look at the world permanently shifts. Usually, these moments come unbidden, when you least expect them. For me, it arrived during a bicycle ride in Phoenix, Arizona, in the spring of 2017.

Biking through the Phoenix Arts District one afternoon while heading back to the color-washed hostel I'd been staying in on Ninth Street, I found myself deep in thought. Balancing my iced coffee in one hand and steering with the other, I let my mind wander. I was a bit awestruck by the afternoon I'd spent at a museum, a visit I'd expected to be insightful but that had also turned out to be deeply moving. For the last several weeks, I'd been indulging in all the goodness Phoenix offered, witnessing how the desert moon rises high, long before sunset. The city was one of many stops on a backpacking trip I'd decided to take the leap on, and I'd just toured the Pueblo Grande Museum and Archeological

Park. The park is home to a replication of a thousand-year-old indigenous village of adobe homes arranged communally in compounds that allowed people to hunt, fish, cook, eat, gather, build, work, play, and celebrate together. The Hohokam people had figured out a way to exist—communally and simply, with intention and innovation—that mirrored what I was craving: a way of life I hadn't yet witnessed but that I deeply longed for. The museum made clear this way of existing had been possible all along and had been achieved with great efficiency in societies past.

As I considered how many other undiscovered ways there must be to live and how many existences I might learn about, honor, and borrow from, I heard my phone ping. Still dreaming of the sloping, sand-colored arches of the Hohokam village that married function and form so beautifully, I pulled over to read a text from a friend. She informed me that a photo of me from the 2017 Washington, D.C., Women's March that had gone viral months before had been posted to the Instagram account of Afropunk, a Black-centered news and cultural commentary outlet.

Several months before, like so many women horrified at the election of Donald Trump, I had made my way to the nation's capital to protest. Along with friend and fellow feminist Dana Suchow, I had organized a busload of women to travel to D.C. and join the voices opposing the misogyny, racism, and xenophobia the Trump administration represented.

That photo of Dana and me—a white woman and a Black woman side by side in front of the Capitol Building, each with a protest sign in one hand and a fist held up to the sky in homage to the iconic photo of Gloria Steinem and Dorothy Pitman Hughes—had made the rounds on social media, thrusting me into a national conversation on feminism. Our signs were the crux of most conversations. Dana's read, PROTECT: BLACK, ASIAN, MUSLIM, LATINX, DISABLED, TRANS, FAT, POOR WOMEN. Mine read, IF YOU DON'T FIGHT FOR ALL WOMEN, YOU FIGHT FOR NO WOMEN. For weeks following the march, that photo had been brandished as a shining example of intersectional feminism and solidarity, with responses to it being quite positive and affirming—but the communities and sites where it had been circulating were frequented mostly by white women.

Afropunk, however, had an almost exclusively Black readership.

I began reading the comments posted there. The responses were starkly different from the celebratory reactions given to us on predominately white platforms. One after another, Afropunk's commenters called out the fallacy of white feminism, questioning why I, a Black woman, was so dedicated to a movement that had never truly been for me. Some of the comments practically shouted for me to open my eyes to the whitewashing and racism of the feminist movement. I felt blindsided and utterly embarrassed at the thought of how much I hadn't known back when I organized the trip to the march, along with a deep sense of responsibility to better understand, to unearth what I hadn't yet discovered.

I will forever be grateful that I happened to be traveling when I got this wake-up call. While I had always known there were flaws in the feminist movement, this moment of realization would send me crashing into a reckoning with the depths of hypocrisy and betrayal in the movement as well as a reckoning with myself. Having only a small suitcase and a backpack to my name, and stripped of familiar surroundings, I was open to what I didn't already know about the world, to different ways of thinking and being. The education I'd just received about the Hohokam people at the Pueblo Grande Museum—completely unknown to me until that day—prepared me for an exploration of what I did and didn't understand about white supremacy and the feminist movement. It began a reimagining of a more honest, more critical worldview.

Over the next several months, I dove into reading, researching, and considering my place in the world more critically, as I'd never really taken the time to do. I dug into the feminist movement, all the way down to its roots, so I could examine what lay beneath. I had to shapeshift my understanding, replacing the whitewashed version of the movement I had once believed accurate with an ugly truth that dismissed both the pain and powerful activism of Black women and other women of color.

Once I learned the truth about the contributions of Black women activists in the fight for women's rights and freedoms—trailblazers like Anna Julia Cooper, Mary Church Terrell, and Ida B. Wells—I studied their blueprints for disrupting the status quo. I realized I had so much to learn from my intellectual ancestors. The truths of the past were opening up a new, more authentic path for me to forge in my own burgeoning activist career.

Inevitably, the process of reexamining *myself* unfolded. I began excavating the depths of who I thought I was and allowing a new version of myself to step forward. I didn't yet have the language or tools for it, but what I was doing was reimagining both myself and the lens through which I viewed the world and its possibilities. It wouldn't be the first time I'd done so, but it was the first time it happened with so much intention and so publicly.

My gut instinct during the whirlwind of these discoveries was to share what I was learning. My social media posts became tools for unlearning what many of us had always taken as truth. As I shared my own personal evolution and the facts I was learning about feminism and racism, my audience grew by tens of thousands, drawing in folks of all stripes who were invested in learning, unlearning, and reimagining alongside me. I became someone people looked to as they explored this intersection of race, womanhood, and identity and considered the possibilities of how we might reimagine it all as we moved forward together. And in 2018 this virtual community expanded to include real-life camaraderie when I kicked off my first public lecture, which I eventually presented all over the country, from North Carolina and Oregon to New England and Los Angeles.

Along the way, I recognized that a critical element of reimagining our totality, within and beyond movement work, is to identify and question the values handed to us by society, our parents, the media, and our educational and economic systems. I began to make room to ask myself: *Is this something I really want to claim? Is there a better way? What can I wield with my hands to exist within my values?*

To answer these questions, I began paying attention to my thoughts and daydreams and noting the experiences that brought me joy or that made me yearn for more. What made me feel grounded, satisfied, energized, and true? With ongoing self-reflection, I discovered and defined my own set of values—values that would supplant those I had inherited from a world shaped by whiteness, capitalism, misogyny, and scarcity. I landed on a trio of guideposts, or what I call my "highest values"—ease, abundance, and opportunity—that became integral to every decision I made thereafter, whether tiny or towering. (You'll spend some time later identifying your own highest values.)

Aligning how I moved through the world with these highest values—and with knowledge, empathy, and action—completely changed how I showed up in my relationships, at work, and for myself. It made space for me to live based not on expectation, routine, or the traditional markers of "success," but on what *I* value most. Encouraged by this clarity, I experimented with new and inspired ways of existing, working, playing, resting, and loving that didn't always line up with what was expected of me.

Through it all, I have reimagined new paths for myself that have allowed me to center in my life both my own wellness and joy and that of my community. I have reimagined myself over and over in order to live fully, to embrace all that I am, both in and beyond the fight for equality (where so much of my work has lived):

> I have reimagined myself as someone who can explore love and sexuality without the rules and limitations mainstream society insists on—chiefly, monogamy and heterosexuality.

I have reimagined myself as someone who is intentionally child-free as opposed to subscribing to a blueprint of womanhood that says one's greatest successes are partnership and parenthood.

I have reimagined my "work," to allow it to happen outside the traditional corporate framework.

I have reimagined my relationship to rest, claiming soft and simple spaces for myself that thwart our society's capitalist mandate to consistently produce.

My highest values—ease, abundance, and opportunity—have boosted my ability to reimagine new ways to learn, love, and exist within and for my community. I've discovered that my work doesn't have to be rooted solely within Black pain and that my activism can be just as powerful with intentions, acts, and experiences that center joy or fulfillment—in other words, struggle isn't the only place where our work must be done.

The simple act of reimagining, of actively reshaping the frameworks you've been handed so that they reflect what you believe they *can* and *should* reflect—a long-standing survival skill for Black women—is incredibly powerful. With this book, my hope is to create space for you to do just that.

In the United States and, one might say, throughout what is perceived as the Western world, women and Black women in particular are rarely afforded the space and resources to flourish. We exist within an infrastructure that purposely and systematically dismisses, oppresses, and exploits us.

Therefore, we *must* reimagine ourselves and our reality; we *must* use the map of our dreams to create new ways of being.

While the process of reimagining is rich with possibility, it would be naïve to suggest that it doesn't carry its own set of challenges. Every reimagining, every decision we make in life, has its shadow side. By shadow side, I am referring to the aspects of a decision that would be listed in the "Cons" column of your pros-and-cons list. No one likes the shadow side of things, but I've grown to view this cloudy side of the street not as a threat, but as an early-warning system, one that allows me to prepare for the inevitable difficult moments and experiences that will naturally unfold as a result of my simply being human. In my own reimagining, I did the calculations of choosing my own path, and I calibrated the shifts I needed to make to compensate for the shadow sides of it all as best as I could. Most important, I felt confident that I had the willingness and ability to adjust along the way.

Shadow sides show up almost everywhere. From the decisions we make around where to live and whom to partner with, to what career we choose and how to spend our time and energy. Reimagining means seeing yourself and your world anew while also reckoning with both the light and shadow of this newness.

A RENAISSANCE OF YOUR OWN

WHEN WE REIMAGINE, WE ARE CREATING THE RUNWAY toward our renaissance. The French word *renaissance* translates to "rebirth" and is most often used to refer to a period in European history after the Middle Ages, when there was an explosion of art, commerce, and discovery. I am using the word *renaissance* in this book to speak to the renewal, or rebirth, of our chosen selves.

When we are born, we are ushered through the world with a set of rules meant to uphold society's status quo. If you live in the United States, your society sits on a foundation of capitalism, white supremacy, and patriarchy. And we can add colonialism to that list for almost the entirety of the Western world, including the United States. As you move toward a renaissance of your own, however, thoughtful consideration of your own values, dreams, and desires will provide you with the rules you should actually be living by.

I want this book to serve as a reminder to you of the power and possibility of reimagining. Not to overthrow the government or start a revolution (although, if that's where your renaissance takes you, I'm here for it) but to live a life that feels right all the way down into the marrow of your bones.

When I was a young activist, my first public reimagining, while painful, fostered a newness, a trueness, in the way I lived from then on. Reimagining has allowed me to bypass the structures I thought I had to exist within, the ones, I was told, I had to build my life around: conventional education systems; traditional relationships; white-centered beauty standards; and standardized approaches to work and to rest and to play.

When I set out to write this book, I embarked on a process not only of sharing what I'd learned, but also of discovery and self-reflection. This book itself is a reimagining, one that revealed itself as I engaged with it. It started out as one thing and then turned into another. I had to stop several times in the process, had to let go of what I *thought* this book was supposed to be and allow it to unfold into what you hold in your hands today. This is what reimagining is, a constant process of observation, curiosity, and intention.

HOW TO USE THIS BOOK

THIS BOOK TELLS MY STORY AND IS ORGANIZED AROUND the themes of life that I have reimagined: faith, relationships, feminism, education, work, and rest. In each chapter, you'll witness my personal transformation and be prompted to reflect on your own. I open this book with my personal manifesto. A manifesto is defined as a declaration of intentions. My manifesto is my road map to reimagining that helps me chart my course in life. But I'd also like you to regard it as a template for creating your own manifesto. At the end of each chapter, I will include a section of the manifesto and will prompt you to replace my values, intentions, and dreams (in boldface) with your own. In so doing, by the end of this book you will have created your own manifesto, one that can forever remind you of the reimagining we've done here and the goals you've set forth for evolving in this lifetime. For some, this book may reflect the path you have been uncovering or trekking for some time now. For others, it might offer a glimpse of what a reimagined life could be. And still for others, it may simply be an opportunity to witness and affirm our shared humanity.

There is something here for all humans—but I want to say that this book is dedicated to Black women. I offer it to you in the hope that these pages will remind you of your birthright to reimagine and inhabit new, liberating mindsets and frameworks. And I hope that in sharing my story I might invite you to join me in reimagining an equitable, authentic, joyful, and deeply satisfying life—for yourself, for your community, and for generations to come. Much of what you read here you will already know deep in your soul and in your body. It is my wish that by giving that shared inner knowledge a voice, I am reaffirming what you know to be true.

Ultimately, I want this book to be a model of living freely. I want it to guide you into a renaissance of your own. I hope my words inspire your own reimagining, that my story might be a spark that lights a fire of some kind of transformation of your own. With that aim in mind, I have included, at the end of each chapter, opportunities for you to actively engage with the ideas presented, through writing prompts, concepts for reflection, and a template to draft a line of your own personal manifesto. Please view these prompts as launching blocks to begin your journey, as springboards for your imagination, and as gentle reminders of what's on the other side of possibility. My intention is that this book will be consumed in a series of reading, writing, and reflecting on your part, so that the ideas presented on these pages have a chance to resonate.

Not everything in this book will apply to every reader; nor should it. I hold a "keep the meat and throw out the bones" approach to life, and I hope you will engage with this book in a similar fashion: Hold on to what speaks to you—

find the good, the useful, the easeful for *you*—and discard what does not. While other people's successes leave clues—I personally study role models' accomplishments like I'm prepping for an exam—the most fulfilling reimaginings happen when you personalize them, make them your own.

I wish you well, dear reader, as you join me in unfolding this renaissance of our own.

CHAPTER 1

REIMAGINING BELIEF SYSTEMS

...

WHILE I WAS GROWING UP, MY FAMILY ATTENDED Antioch Baptist Church, on the west side of Akron, Ohio, each and every Sunday. During my elementary school years, I rode a bus to a tiny, private, white suburban Christian school where, every week, we memorized a new Bible verse. It's safe to say, no matter the environment, I was steeped in the Church for most of my early life. In fact, Christianity was *the* moral compass of my household for many years, and church was the cornerstone of our schedules. Each Sunday, we'd file out of the church, where the membership was made up of both family and friends. These were the people I sold Girl Scout Cookies to each spring, whom I turned to for references when applying for my first job. Church was part of the ritual and rhythm of my young life.

I was born and raised in a small suburban town right outside Akron. The town was called Green, like the color, and green it was. There were towering evergreen trees and manicured lawns on every block. My family lived on a cul-de-sac at the end of a two-way street in a tight-knit neighborhood.

Bright yellow speed bumps served as after-school balance beams as well as they slowed the cars that came down our way. There was a massive field near our house where the neighborhood kids would gather to play tag or soccer or sometimes just to lie among the dandelions.

Though Green was populated with modest homes, our area was surrounded by more affluent neighborhoods, with newly built houses boasting four and five bedrooms and two-car garages. Huge stone signs at the front of these gated communities bore aspirational British-sounding names like "Prestwick" and "Mayfair."

Despite the affluence surrounding us, my family was poor. We lived in a two-story, three-bedroom townhouse connected to a complex of similar apartments and town-homes. The house had just enough space for our family: my parents and, with my birth, three girls. While I was my mother's third child, I was the first and only child she had with my father. By the time I was born, my sisters were already preteens—Michelle, twelve, and April, eleven.

In my earliest remembering, I had no idea that we were poor or that my mother could afford the life we had only with the help of government assistance. Our townhouse was classified as Section 8 housing, and food stamps and welfare checks supplied our basic needs. Of course, as a little girl, this meant nothing to me. I knew only that I had a nice, modest home, a yard to play in, and two parents who loved me. And this was by design.

My mother was one of six children born into a lower-class Black family who possessed no blueprint for improving their circumstances. An outlier among her siblings, she recognized that raising her children in the same inner-city neighborhood on the west side of Akron where she'd grown up, and where the rest of her family continued to languish, was not going to help her daughters boost their station in life. But my mother bore the additional burden of having contracted polio at age five, unable to walk without the aid of crutches thereon. This restricted her ability to work outside the home. Still, knowing that her choices were limited, she made the decision to look for affordable housing in the suburbs rather than stay in a crowded, dingy apartment complex—the kind the city housing authority was notoriously known to offer Black women with dependent children. By moving us to Green, my mother curated a life for us that allowed us to bear witness to what was possible. She created her own blueprint for changing her family's fortunes.

Despite her physical disability, my mother was fiercely independent. She'd always be there, in that first row of the bleachers, cheering me on in my soccer games, and she attended as many of my Girl Scout camping trips as possible. While work outside the home wasn't always an option for her, she consistently found ways to supplement what little government support we received—more often than not, while in service to the community. She tutored kids in the neighborhood, sold beautiful homemade greeting cards in the local hospital gift shop, and created a reading program at the daycare my aunt owned. My mother was industrious and creative, and she was always preparing me for a better life, a life she herself never experienced. She enrolled me in etiquette classes and golf lessons, sent me to that private Christian school, and she always reminded me, with pride in her voice, "Rachel, even though we don't have a lot of money, we *look* like we do."

My father didn't share my mother's work ethic. He never kept a steady job and he came with both a financial and emotional unavailability that my mother bore the weight of. He lived with us until I was ten years old, but my parents weren't married, and I'm not even sure I could say that they were ever in love. Nonetheless, he had a powerful impact on my young life, making me feel loved and secure.

My father's kindness, laughter, and warmth stood in stark contrast to my mother's more stoic personality. She took a no-nonsense approach to life and seemed to think emotions were most often excessive. "You'll be okay" was what she usually said to me when I brought home any childhood slight or pain. Even positive emotions seemed too much for her. Still, while she wasn't demonstrative with her affection in the way my father was, I never doubted her love for me.

In those early days, the glue that held my family together the most was survival, survival, and Jesus.

DEVOTION AND DISRUPTION

LIKE MOST BAPTISTS, WE BELIEVED THAT JESUS DIED FOR our sins and that the only way to get to heaven—the ultimate goal in life for a devoted Baptist—was to believe that He was both Lord and Savior. Without Christ, there was no salvation. As a child, I understood that being a good Christian meant following the rules my mother and grandmother meted out, going to church, and loving God and His Holy Son. Through church, we were also taught that it was our personal responsibility to build our own relationship with God through study and prayer. So my family didn't go to church *only* on Sundays. As soon as my sisters and I were old enough to pass the collection plate, *additional* participation in one ministry or another was expected of us. Also, our mother taught Vacation Bible School every summer, and of course I was expected to attend.

But I didn't mind one bit. I actually loved spending time at church as a child. Church was my safe space and reprieve. It was where I got to play with my Black friends and be a part of a wider Black family, which was a welcome contrast to my mostly white suburban existence. It was the place where I felt most like myself when I was little. It was at church—jumping double Dutch; clapping hands with other little Black girls, singing "Miss Mary Mack"—where I truly felt like a happy Black child.

Some Saturdays, my cousins and I would spend the night at our grandma's house. When we'd wake on Sunday morning, Grandma would unfurl the curls she'd pinned our hair into the night before, help us into frilly dresses and socks with lace and bows, and take us to the early-morning Sunday school class. Afterward, we'd sit through the regular ten A.M. service. Then it was back to Grandma's to change out of our fancy clothes and play in her backyard.

That was my life for most of my early childhood years. It wasn't perfect, but it seemed pretty normal. We had family dinners where my dad made everyone laugh. We went to church on Sundays. We seemed to be doing as well as we could.

And then everything changed.

ON THE NIGHT OF her senior prom, my sister Michelle returned home with another life within her. My niece Schuyler was born when I was seven. In an attempt to take responsibility for her life and actions, Michelle moved into an apartment in the city shortly after Schuyler's birth.

Not long after, after graduating from high school, April also moved out, as she moved into adulthood and began to manage an unexpected pregnancy of her own.

But as my elder sisters were growing up and beginning their adult lives, I gained a new little sister, Myriah, when my older cousin became incarcerated and my mother decided to bring her infant daughter to live with us, rather than see her shuttled through the foster care system.

It was during this era of change that my mother asked my father to leave the house. He wasn't bringing enough to the table to make it worthwhile to support him any further, especially not as she was taking on another mouth to feed. While I still saw my father, it was certainly not the same as having him in our home.

It seemed that my world was being flipped upside down. Although my mother had been shouldering the responsibility of running our family affairs all along, we were now officially a single woman–led household. And then what was left of my "normal childhood" was cruelly taken away.

JUST A YEAR AFTER HE'D LEFT OUR HOME, MY FATHER was diagnosed with kidney failure, and there was a short period during which he returned to live in our home so my mother and I could care for him.

I'd grown up believing in miracles, and those early Bible stories gave my young belief proof. So, as I watched my father grow weaker and skinnier, I did as I'd been taught to do every Sunday: I took my burdens to the Lord. I prayed that my father would be the recipient of one of those miracles and that I'd be right there when he received it.

But his care proved to be too much for my mom to handle, and she made what I believe to have been the hard choice of placing him in a nursing home. He spent the last months of his life deteriorating in that place. After school, I'd go sit by his bed and read, hoping my voice and presence would cheer him up, simply happy to be with him.

At the time, I didn't truly understand that he was dying. My mother's stoic nature made it hard for me to read whether this was the end, or just a critical part of my father's journey, one he would get past. Regardless, I faithfully showed up to share that space and time with him. I believed healing could happen.

But my father didn't get better. Just shy of two years after his diagnosis, his ailing body succumbed. I was devastated. In so many ways, I'd lost my best friend.

Today, there is an incredibly empty place inside me where sadness at my father's passing should reside. I was heartbroken when he died, certainly, but back then, my mother didn't have the capacity to manage my emotions along with everything else going on in the household, so I forced my sadness down and away until it remained unseen.

I didn't witness my mother's grief. She may have grieved in private, but the truth was our household had become so utterly consumed with the increasingly troubled, chaotic lives of my older sisters that pausing for grief wasn't an option: For reasons I was too young to understand and still, today, cannot truly comprehend, both my sisters became victims of addiction, one to alcohol and one to drugs, and we bore witness as their lives collapsed into dysfunction and pain. Within a very short space of time, each lost custody of her children, and my mother and I had to step in.

Together my mother and I shouldered the responsibility of raising April's two children and helping out with Michelle's, all of them traumatized by their mothers' addictions, which had rapidly spiraled out of control. From the time I was eleven years old, our lives felt like a revolving door of visits with social service agencies, trips to rehabilitation centers, drop-ins from law enforcement, and broken promises from my sisters, two women I used to adore. And because my mother was disabled, she depended on me to do much of the physical work now required to care for two extra kids, not to mention Myriah and myself. Grocery shopping, running errands, school pick-up on snowy Ohio days when conditions were too dangerous for a woman dependent on crutches to be out on the road. It all fell to me.

As I matured into adolescence, I developed deep resentment and anger toward my sisters for the choices they had made and the pain they'd caused our family, particularly our mother. I also felt a deep sense of obligation to be a dutiful daughter to my mother, to stay with her to continue helping her raise my sisters' children, and to keep an eye on her. Despite my most fervent desire to flee from the madness that defined my home life, college just wasn't an option. The thought of leaving my mother alone to handle Myriah, my niece, and my nephew while I went off to college felt irresponsible. So, for most of my high school years, while I watched friends make plans for college, I set my goals somewhat lower.

I always assumed I would take custody of April's children, raising them myself when my mother's advanced age and weakened health would make her ability to continue to do so impossible. In fact, I spent much of high school with my mind on a loop, lost in thoughts of how I might care for the kids while also financially supporting my mother. I pondered how I could apply for affordable government housing and still pursue a professional life, one that wouldn't cause me to lose that housing.

My heart aches today thinking about that version of myself who believed she was responsible for so many people. And yet, even at that young age, I still reasoned that, if *this* was to be my fate, to stay stuck in a system of dependence like the rest of my family, I would do it differently. If ending up in the welfare system was how my life was going to turn out, I decided, then I was going to be the most efficient person I could be within that system. I would be on top of whatever paperwork and appointments were required of me, I told myself. I would work the system to the best of my ability. My house would be the nicest, the most well-kept house in whatever housing project I ended up in. Looking back on it now, I see that I was reaching for whatever good fruit I could find to pick off the blighted little tree I felt I had been assigned in life.

But even then—with my life seemingly defined by struggle, drama, and chaos—I had an inkling of the power I possessed to have something better. And thanks to my mother's insistence that we "look like we have money," I understood how to hide the reality of my home life so I could slip into that version of life that existed beyond the walls of our home.

In some ways, you could say, this was the very beginning of my life of reimagining.

DESPITE ALL I WAS dealing with at home, I projected a carefree, joyous countenance, and it was easy for me to make friends with the mostly white, more affluent kids at my middle school and high school. I would use my time at school, soccer practices, and birthday party sleepovers to research what else was possible. It was in these places that I got the chance to peek into the ways other people were able to live in the world.

I desperately paid attention, asked all the questions, and inserted myself into as many opportunities as I could to try to experience this "better" way of life. This was my first rodeo with the ways white supremacy warps our perception of what a "good life" is and what we should all aspire to. I found myself equating everything my white friends had with things *I* should want, too.

And while the difference between my white friends' home life and mine was stark, I was still grateful for the opportunity and the access to see beyond what my mother could offer me. My mother had believed that raising her children outside the inner city would be enough for them to escape the social ills that plagued her family tree, but it obviously was not. Not for my sisters at least. But for me, it was a start. It was enough to show me that government assistance wasn't the only way to live. That I didn't have to repeat the cycle of early and unexpected pregnancy. That I didn't have to resort to drugs and alcohol to dull the pain of bad decisions and broken promises.

COLLEGE BOUND

WHILE MY MOTHER HAD DONE HER BEST TO RESCUE ME from the world she'd grown up in, she didn't know how to launch me beyond our home. When I expressed my intention to stay home and forgo college to help her take care of the children, she dismissed the idea as nonsense and told me I *had* to go. But figuring out *how* to get me to college was not in her bag of tricks. Luckily she knew someone who could help.

I had a cousin, Monica, who not only finished college, but would eventually go on to procure her Ph.D. Even though, by this time, it was rather late in my high school career to start planning for college, my mom said we'd figure it out and turned my future over to Monica, who helped me apply to the University of Toledo, a state school in Ohio that met my mother's criterion that the school not be too far away, and my own, that I needed to know one other person who went there. With my solid academic record and all my extracurricular activities, Monica was confident I would be accepted. And she was right. I got in.

In the fall, when it was time for me to leave home, my mother drove me the two hours to Toledo. We stopped at a Walmart on the way to grab whatever basic supplies I would need to outfit my dorm room and that my mom could afford. It all felt slightly surreal. Sure, I wasn't going far, but I *was* going.

When we arrived at the dorms, my mother stayed in the car while I unloaded everything at the curb. We said goodbye through the car window, and I expressed my gratitude for the ride to my next chapter. As much as I attempted to look confident being left alone at the steps of my college dorm, the fear I was feeling must have shown on my face. (Despite my mother's best efforts to make me as unflappable and unburdened by emotion as she was, it had never worked.)

"You'll be fine, Rachel. You'll have a good time. Now go on and get your room set up."

And with that, she turned the car around and headed home.

I ARRIVED AT THE University of Toledo as an overwhelmed seventeen-year-old, feeling utterly alone, becoming one of twenty thousand students on the suburban campus trying to figure it all out. So, when I was invited to join a Christian student group within the first week of my arrival, I happily said yes to the offer of community and companionship—and quickly and easily fell in step with this welcoming group of Black students. Like me, they had grown up in the Church, and also like me, they were facing college without a large financial safety net or a legacy of generations of family members who had gone to college before them. We spoke the same language, had the same roots, and wanted the same things out of life.

Soon enough, this group became the center of my social life, and thus, my social life became centered on church once again. Every week, my friends and I would gather for Bible study, and after Bible study, we'd all have dinner together. There were gospel choir practices on Friday nights—I would come to watch; my voice was never choir material—church on Sunday mornings, and then a brunch that always folded into dinner. Sometimes, a bunch of us would get together at our pastor's house, at his invitation, for a meal and some unstructured socializing. I felt loved, comforted, and supported. I had found a home away from home.

Thanks to my church friends, my confidence grew, and I started to explore more of the UT campus. I volunteered at the Women's Center. I applied and participated in things like the Freshman Leadership Program and joined the board of the Student United Way. I went to parties and met exciting new people. I declared a major in social work and started thinking about a future that included law school and a job advocating for the needs of the Black community in some capacity.

I didn't know exactly how it would all turn out, but I was enjoying myself immensely at college, free for the first time to explore all my interests; to put myself first without worrying about my sisters, my nieces and nephews, or even my mother. After just one year of college, I was already falling in love with the person I was becoming.

A GOOD CHRISTIAN MAN

IT WAS A CRISP, SUNNY DAY IN JANUARY, THE BEGINNING of the second semester of my sophomore year, when I first laid eyes on Manny. At the invitation of a recent gospel choir acquaintance, I was visiting a new church with friends and looking forward to the whole experience. After the service, a group of us stood around laughing and chatting in the church parking lot, debating where to grab a meal and hang out a bit before the school week descended upon us once again.

Holding court in the middle of one small crowd was Manny, dark-skinned with a beautiful smile and dimples in both cheeks. He was a little shorter than my own five foot nine, but he was so charismatic that he didn't need the extra height to stand out. Manny held everyone's attention.

We locked eyes several times, pretending to be in deep conversation with our respective friends but obviously aware of each other. By the end of an evening filled with jokes and shared stories over an early dinner, I discovered that Manny went to Bowling Green State University, about fifteen miles away from Toledo. He was in the Air National Guard, was one of six children, loved his church, and wanted my phone number.

I was intrigued: He seemed like perfect boyfriend material. Namely, he seemed solid, safe, and kind. The fact that he was a Christian also gave me comfort, as it signified that he had a moral code and an upbringing I had been taught to value.

So, I gave him my phone number.

A few multi-hour phone calls and conversations at the back of the university library turned into a few dates at the local bookstore and Saturday mornings out for breakfast. Eventually, as Valentine's Day rolled around, it was evident that Manny and I had a connection we wanted to explore more intentionally.

Things progressed quickly. Manny was grounded, good-hearted, and ready for a serious relationship. And he was infatuated with me. He'd snap pictures of me when I wasn't looking, eagerly offer me rides to and from my part-time job, make the dark Ohio winter treks to spend a few hours with me on my campus, and frequently let me know he found me beautiful and interesting. After about three months of dating, he brought up the idea of marriage—more specifically, marrying me.

We were sitting in two wooden chairs across from each other inside Carlson Library, so close that I could feel the pheromones pinging back and forth between us. We were knee to knee, both leaning in, our faces close together as he initiated the most intimate conversation I'd ever had.

"What would you think of us getting married, Rachel?"

Even though we'd been seeing each other for only a few months, the question didn't surprise me. Marrying young, rather than going through a prolonged period of dating first, was what people did in Manny's traditional apostolic church community. What *did* surprise me was that the thought of marrying Manny didn't scare me. I really considered the question with intention. I knew, rationally, that Manny was a sweet and caring man and that marrying him would provide me with a soft, safe place to land. But right on the heels of that realization came another: I was flooded with thoughts of my previous relationship just the year before.

His name was Marcus, and he had set my mind and body aflame during the nine-month freshman-year rendezvous we shared. Marcus was my first taste of uninhibited passion as I veered away from what I had been taught to desire. I found him intellectually intriguing, and he opened up a world of intimacy I never knew existed. We would spend hours in his room, hiding away from the frat brothers he lived with—reading books to each other, debating politics in the lead-up to Obama's election in 2008, skipping class to have indulgent sex, and engaging in casual conversation over cups of hot tea.

But Marcus had been a senior, and I was just a freshman. He didn't want to marry me or even commit to a real relationship. He was simply one of my first departures from what a "good Christian relationship" should mimic in terms of acting on our desires. While I was able to bite the bullet and move on from what felt like loss when Marcus and I called it quits, what we had—the passion, the excitement—was what I wanted in a marriage.

So, while Manny demonstrated other, really beautiful qualities that attracted me to him, I didn't yet feel that same level of exhilaration that Marcus had provided and what I had mistakenly taken as a "truer" love.

I tried to explain this to Manny. "I adore you," I started. "But my feelings for you don't feel like what I want lifelong love to feel like."

Manny didn't flinch. "Rachel, I hear what you're saying, but the Bible tells us that we can't trust our feelings when making critical life decisions like this. Feelings fluctuate. And sometimes our feelings are based on other things besides the truth."

"I guess so."

While the Church hadn't been as deeply foundational in my own life as it had been for Manny, I understood and wanted to believe in the veracity of Christian doctrine. It was enticing to believe that there was a clear right and wrong, good and evil, saint and sinner. I wanted to believe that Manny was working with biblical knowledge I wasn't aware of, so I assumed his words and beliefs held more weight than mine. After all, I was simply basing my ideas on how one flaky frat boy named Marcus had made me feel.

I decided it would be "wiser" to trust Manny more than I trusted myself.

"I've really been praying about this," Manny said then. "And I think this is what's right for us."

When he said that, I felt something inside me begin to lean toward the idea, to grasp the notion of a possible future in a traditional, stable marriage—even if it felt way too soon.

"Okay," I said. "Let's start considering it."

For the rest of the semester and throughout the summer, Manny and I continued to get to know each other. I found him really funny and kind, and I loved spending time with him and his large family. When I was in the mix, they happily embraced me and treated me as family. With both his parents being ministers themselves, I also began to grow further in my Christian faith, through deeper reading of the Bible, prayer, and dialoguing with Manny's family members. The very faith that had wavered at times throughout my childhood and adolescence became the quickest way to settle into a possible life with Manny.

Manny was a salve for so many of the pain points I had developed while growing up. Whenever he could, he would show me how responsible and caring he could be, something I found deeply attractive. Once, at the end of the semester, I worked a full-day shift at my job and I was stressed because I had to get my dorm room packed up and emptied by the next day. But I simply couldn't afford to miss a day's worth of pay. I confessed all this to Manny on the phone as I rushed off to work—and sure enough, I arrived back at my room that night to discover that he had organized and packed up everything. I was so grateful, and his gesture filled me with such a sense of peace and joy. Growing up in a household where so much had fallen on my shoulders simply because I was the most capable person in the family had made me particularly appreciative of a partner who could do more than me and who had no problem helping me out.

I was so appreciative that a high-functioning, disciplined, and resourceful person was in my life and was attracted to me as well! So, whenever my treacherous little heart reminded me that I wasn't madly, deeply in love with Manny, I would tell myself that a "normal" home life, one that was stable, free from drama, and built on the foundations of the Christian faith was so much better than some fantasy version of romantic love.

Manny's family all lived in Dayton, Ohio, about a two-hour drive from Toledo, and we'd often go down to visit them and their church family. I reveled in the wholesomeness of these visits—a true departure from my family gatherings, where my cousins' idea of a good time always included smoking, drinking, and getting high. I knew Manny's parents would have preferred that I'd grown up apostolic, but they liked me enough, and they saw that I was willing to be involved with their church and follow their rules.

When Manny and I visited his parents, I'd have to stay with one of his sisters, as it was considered inappropriate for Manny and me to stay in the same house overnight. (On our own, Manny and I had decided not to have sex until after we were married.) Since I thought of Manny's sisters as my friends by this point, the rule didn't bother me much. I was enjoying being a part of such a large, faith-based family.

The only thing that bothered me was that small, nagging feeling in my gut that kept signaling to me that marrying Manny wasn't the best choice for me.

But I didn't listen to my gut. In fact, I fought it aggressively. Just because my stomach wasn't full of butterflies for Manny, I couldn't come up with a *practical* reason not to marry him. We had a strong friendship, an easy way of being together, and meaningful conversations, and he had proven to me time and time again his deep commitment to me, his work ethic, and his sense of responsibility. We were very attracted to each other, and everyone in our social circles kept reaffirming our union.

"Manny is such a catch," my girlfriends told me.

"Rachel will be such a great wife," Manny's friends told him.

We were a golden couple within our respective church groups, and our getting married seemed like an affirmation of everything we had been led to believe was our destiny as "good

Christians." There weren't any red flags indicating real danger ahead. On the contrary, marrying Manny seemed like the fulfillment of all my ideas about what a successful marriage looked like based on the ones I saw growing up, on TV and in the homes of my friends whose lives I'd studied so closely.

There was another thing. Just the *idea* of being Manny's wife granted me an unshakeable sense of safety. And, dear reader, you must understand that my need for safety at this point in my life cannot be understated. Here I was, barely a woman, on her own in an unknown environment after surviving a chaotic and traumatizing childhood that included the death of her father; a disabled and, at times, sickly mother; two sisters in the ugly throes of addiction; coparenting her nieces and nephews alongside her mother, all the while teetering on the edge of poverty. *Safety* and *security* were two words that had played no part in my childhood.

But I knew that once I became a part of Manny's world, that sense of security and safety I'd always craved would be made manifest as I was welcomed into his large, loving, high-functioning family. I told myself I should feel lucky that this really lovely man had been moved to propose to me. And I can't deny that I was also approaching the idea of marriage from a space of wonder and worry: *What if this is the only man who will ever find me worth proposing to? What if I miss out on my only opportunity to be a wife?* Consciously and unconsciously, I allowed the pressure society had put on me—the same it puts on most women—to view marriage as the ultimate win to factor into my decision.

When Manny asked me again if I was ready to get married, just five months after introducing the idea, I said yes.

Once the decision was made, getting married meant taking practical steps. Neither of us had any money, so instead of an extravagant, overpriced wedding, Manny and I went to the courthouse in Dayton, accompanied by his mom and one of his sisters, and stood up for a civil ceremony. It was 2009. I wore a yellow sundress. Manny chose khakis and a button-down shirt. I got my hair styled for the occasion, but other than that, after all my mental machinations, the day felt rather anticlimactic. But I was happy to finally have everything settled and to be Manny's wife.

After the ceremony, Manny's family and friends joined us for a celebration dinner at the local Red Robin, home of "America's Gourmet Burgers and Spirits." No one from my side of the family came to our celebration. My mother couldn't make it down to Dayton—she didn't have the money or means to ensure that my niece and nephew would be cared for in her absence—and I don't know if my sisters even knew I'd become a wife. Truth be told, not having my family at my wedding actually felt appropriate, as marrying Manny signified that I was moving on and creating my own family, one that would be reflective of our Christian values and the American Dream.

A GOOD CHRISTIAN WOMAN

ONCE WE WERE MARRIED, MANNY AND I DECIDED TO withdraw from our respective universities to get settled in his hometown of Dayton, where we planned to live long term. I fully intended to return to school, but I needed to figure out how to pay for it, as I'd run out of money and didn't want to take on any more loans.

Right after the wedding, we moved into a cheap, tiny, worn-down one-bedroom basement apartment near his family and got busy putting our plans in place for the future. In the beginning, Manny worked at the local Best Buy while serving in the military as a reservist for the air force. Meanwhile, I worked part time as an administrative assistant at the daycare his mother owned. We were the quintessential struggling young couple. Our couch was a repurposed hand-me-down, and our bed was one we found on the street and dragged home. Without enough money for entertainment or extras, we'd spend our evenings talking about our future, watching *The Fresh Prince of Bel Air*, having "just married" sex, and eating the only dinner we could afford most nights: chocolate chip pancakes and bacon. We were cozy, happy, and enjoying our time together.

And yet, some days, while Manny was at work, I'd find myself huddled in the back pew of a random church I'd snuck off to, sobbing and begging God to remove the insistent pang in my gut telling me Manny wasn't the one for me. I was so confused. How could I have a wonderful man by my side, a loving extended family, and a pathway to a safe and comfortable future but still feel that something was wrong? Most days, I'd wake up feeling like I was at the peak of a roller-coaster incline, just waiting for the bottom to drop out. The agony of this ever-present sense of discontent robbed me of the peace I'd been searching for.

Dear God, I'd pray, tears streaming down my cheeks, my eyes squeezed shut. *Please take away this awful feeling. Please let me enjoy all the blessings you've given me. I know Manny is a good man, and I can have a good life with him. If this is the Devil trying to steal my joy, please make me strong enough to resist him.*

Before I'd thread through the pews to leave the church, I'd let the Lord know I was open to any clarity He had for me. I would beg God to get rid of the confusion licking at my consciousness. I would will myself to love Manny whole-heartedly and to believe in the vision of the future we were building together. And then I would dry my tears, make my way home, and start frying the bacon for our dinner.

Luckily, there was a lot to distract me from my confusion and doubt. By the time October rolled around, I was packing my bags and getting ready to head to Texas for basic training in the air force. Yes, you read that correctly. I was once in the U.S. Air Force. Manny and I had decided that the most effective way for me to continue paying for college, get health benefits, and contribute to our family finances would be through the military. I chose to be practical, to follow in my husband's footsteps and make the air force work for me. By promising to serve for six years, I would earn tuition benefits, healthcare, and other forms of a safety net that weren't otherwise available. I kept my mind open and tried to look at what lay ahead as another opportunity to learn something new and see more of the United States.

Basic training was in San Antonio, at Lackland Air Force Base. I was there for a grueling eight-week initiation into the ranks. It was physically exhausting, but even more mentally taxing. On top of the violent mission and culture of the military, the base itself was rife with racism, sexism, and any

other "ism" you can imagine. I survived the experience, pushing myself past every limit I thought I had, and graduated
training right before the Christmas holiday. Even though it
was back to our shoddy little apartment, I was happy to be
home and safe with my husband.

Manny had prepared me well for what to expect in the
military and I looked at it as simply a means to an end, a way
for Manny and me to continue to build stability in our lives.
Manny planned to take on even more advanced leadership
training at the base, which would result in a substantial up-
grade to our income, but I intended to return to university
after I completed the remainder of my military courses. Because the Guard units aren't on active duty, my commitment
to serve for those six years required that I show up on base
only one weekend a month in addition to one full week a
year. This left space for me to continue my education and
look forward to one day having children and building our
home and family life. This was "the dream," and it felt so
responsible, respectable, and safe. All I had to do was do my
part.

That's what I kept telling myself.

Right on schedule, by the time I finished the second half of
my military training, Manny went from working at Best Buy
to earning a nearly six-figure salary with his new job on the
base in Dayton. By combining my five-figure bonus check
from completing my training with Manny's new salary, we
were able to leave behind our basement dwelling and move
into a really nice two-story apartment in a neighborhood
right on the outskirts of Dayton. We filled it with rented

furniture and checked off a few more boxes on our life plan. With my military tuition benefits, I enrolled at Wright State University and began working as an office manager at the local Jewish daycare center. Manny bought himself a BMW and me a Volkswagen Jetta. We were only about a year and a half into our marriage and on track for so much of what we had dreamt up together.

Less than a year later, Manny and I bought a brand-new three-bedroom house where we were able to select the interior specifics—wall colors, bathroom tiles, kitchen fixtures. I loved it. All of it. Manny took care of our finances, and all I had to do was choose what I wanted our sunroom to look like.

By the time we moved into our perfectly designed house, I decided to stop working—except for my once-a-month commitment to the air force. Financially, there was no need for me to work, and Manny was happy to support us both. I was enjoying having the freedom to do whatever I wanted to do all day and take care of the home. Honestly, I enjoyed being a housewife. I'd cook, clean, and be around for when the landscaper came to take care of the lawn. I finally had some time to consider what I really wanted to do within the framework of the life Manny and I had built.

I started out by increasing my commitment to the Church, hosting weekly Bible Book Club meetings with friends at our house. I then founded a group called Chicks for Charity with my good friend Candace, hosting events and sending the profits to the charities around our small city we were excited to support. Manny and I adopted a minia-

ture schnauzer named Stella, and our life continued to unfold according to plan.

But all was not well in paradise. The nagging doubt in my
gut was still present; I was just getting better at ignoring it.
Even more concerning—left to my own devices all day long,
I was developing curiosity for what else the world had to
offer, and I was intrigued. As social media began to emerge,
I was suddenly seeing women doing bigger and bolder things
than my Midwest experience could have ever exposed me to.
Our perfect Christian family dream life slowly began to feel
very small.

I remember watching hours of, for me, newly discovered
TED Talks while folding laundry, listening to interviews
with trailblazing businesswomen on podcasts while I did the
dishes. I started reading books about business and ethical
entrepreneurship suggested to me by the people I was meeting through my charity work—and something inside me
connected deeply to all of it. I had an inkling that my natural
curiosity, intelligence, and leadership skills could do more
than just act out "the dream" of being a wife and running a
household. Suddenly, at the age of twenty-one, I found that
the world beyond what I had planted in Ohio was beckon-
ing me to explore it.

"Manny, wouldn't it be nice if we moved to somewhere
like Washington, D.C., or New York?" I said one Saturday
evening after dinner. We were snuggling on the sofa in front
of the fireplace, enjoying our first fire of the season.

Manny made a face. "Why would we move? Everything
we need is here. Our family. My job. The house."

"What about medical school?" I asked, knowing the military had expressed interest in his attending its medical school in Washington. I also knew that medical school on the military's dime would probably be the only way to convince my husband to leave Ohio.

"Rachel," Manny said, turning to me with a slow smile. "I don't know if medical school is really for me. Besides, things here are working out so well for us now."

I let out a slight sigh and tried not to fixate on the image in my mind: of me trapped in a cage and Manny holding the key.

Manny seemed to sense my disappointment. "Rachel," he said, gathering me up in a hug. "You are such a brilliant and intelligent woman. You don't need to go to some big city to shine. You can do that here in Ohio, surrounded by people who love you and who will support you in whatever you decide to do."

In response, I gave him the type of smile and sigh that translate as "Yeah, I guess you're right," but inside I felt defeated.

Every few weeks, over the next year, we'd revisit some version of that conversation. Each time, I'd feel smaller and smaller. More deflated and less like a co-creator of the life we were building. But as strong as my frustrations were, I was also afraid that I might be wrong. Plus, I was swimming in guilt over questioning a marriage built on the faith I had been taught to revere and that so closely mirrored mainstream culture's image of perfection. To make matters worse, what I yearned for in its stead didn't even have a name or a destination. I just wanted *more*. More *what*? I couldn't articulate. So, I continued trying to convince myself that what I had was enough.

But I couldn't.

Between the persistent nagging in my gut and the feelings of dismissal when I tried to dream out loud with my husband, I grew increasingly unsettled. Yet I still couldn't rid myself of the sense of shame and nagging fear that washed over me whenever I even entertained the idea of walking away from my marriage. In fact, feeling this way made me desperate to try to find someone who could convince me that I would be crazy to leave only to march off into the unknown. Luckily, Manny had picked up on my feelings of discontent, and on the cusp of our third year as husband and wife, we both agreed to get marriage counseling.

Together, Manny and I decided on a Christian therapist whose office was near our home. I felt hopeful going into the process, but my hopes were quickly dashed when the therapist revealed herself to be irrationally one-sided. Manny got nods and smiles when he spoke of the "straight and narrow" life path he was on while working so hard to build a future for us whereas I received squinted eyes and questioning looks when I mentioned anything that didn't fit into that picture. During our individual sessions, the therapist would ask me, "Do you know how lucky you are to have him? Do you know everything he's given you?" without any consideration for the lack of fulfillment I was voicing or the difficulty Manny and I were having in finding a compromise. She telegraphed that I, as a good Christian woman, should have been grateful to have a good Christian man in the first place.

I'll admit: That's what I had *wanted* to hear, but it did nothing to change my mind. If anything, it made me more resolute in finally listening to what my gut and heart were telling me instead of seeking further outside validation of my own desires.

Shortly after our several-months-long attempt at counseling, I decided to honor the truth my body had been telling me for the last three years: Our marriage was good, but it wasn't right for me. And if it wasn't right for me, that meant it wasn't right for Manny, either.

I remember walking Stella around our neighborhood one morning, strolling past the posh homes where white folks in their forties were living their best lives, and the truth crystalized in my mind: I wasn't living *my* best life. And in that moment, I also knew that if I didn't allow myself the chance to come up for air, I would drown. It wasn't that I was falling *out* of love with Manny; I was simply falling *in* love with myself, coming into a relationship with my truth. I knew I had to give myself the opportunity to discover that fullness, to breathe my own air.

One morning, not long after these heart-wrenching realizations, Manny woke up and kissed me, as he always did. But before he could slip out the bedroom door and leave for work, I looked him in the eye and said, "I really need to talk."

Perhaps it was the tone of my voice, but it was clear that he knew what was coming. I saw the devastation in his eyes, but his stoic nature wouldn't let him get too emotional. I explained how heartbroken I was to be leaving my best friend and this lovely life we had built together. I told him he deserved someone who loved him deeper than I could find the capacity to. I knew I was breaking his heart, but that was our truth—he deserved more, and I did, too.

He called his boss: "I won't be coming in today."

Then we sat down at the kitchen table and wrote out a document that divided everything we'd built together over the last three years. At the time, my feelings were that Manny had worked really hard for what we had, so I told him, "You can keep everything you've earned. Just let me keep my car and a bit of money to cushion me until I figure out an income of my own." He agreed without argument, and as I slipped my wedding ring off my finger and slid it across that smooth wooden table, I was flooded with the bittersweetness of both deep relief and unimaginable fear. The moment felt like both an exhale of having made the decision that had been pulling at my gut for longer than I wanted to admit and an inhale in preparation for what was waiting for me on the other side of all this.

Later that afternoon, I called my mother to let her know the decision I'd made and asked if I could come home to recalibrate. Of course, she said yes. So, I packed up my small Jetta with a few suitcases, my favorite books, and my trusted crockpot and drove away.

The emotional force of what I'd just done hit me once I was on the road. That two-hour stretch of highway back home lives in my head as a whirlwind of devastation and heartbreak for both Manny and me. While I knew that some of my tears were shed in relief, I was also mourning the loss of what I had hoped would be forever.

As soon as I arrived in Akron, I drove straight to Antioch

Baptist Church. It was Wednesday, so I knew my grandmother would be teaching an evening Bible study class and that my mother would be in attendance. I parked my car in the lot, right next to my grandma's teal Oldsmobile, and tiptoed into the sanctuary, where my grandmother was just finishing up her lesson. I slid into a seat at the back of the room and waited for her students to disperse. While I sat there nibbling on a fingernail, I wondered if my mother had already told my grandmother that I was coming home because I'd left my husband. I knew my grandmother wouldn't want to see me suffer through a bad marriage, but she wasn't a fan of divorce, as it went against her Christian values.

Once everyone started to file out, I made my way slowly toward the front of the sanctuary, where my mother was seated and my grandmother was still standing, shuffling her papers together. I hugged my mother first and then turned to greet my grandmother.

"Hi, Grandma," I said, willing the tears to stay put behind my eyelids. I was trembling a bit, both from fear of her rejection and the residual adrenaline of having made one of the hardest decisions of my life. I'll never, ever forget the hug she gave me at that moment. Hers was a particular kind of affirming and unexpected love, and it was exactly what I needed.

After the hug, she looked at me and softly asked, "Are you sure you're done?"

"Yes." I sniffed, falling deeper into her embrace.

She hugged me even tighter, making sure to relay to me that I was going to be okay.

My grandma showing up for me in that moment changed

how I was able to show up for myself. She made space for me to acknowledge the gritty nuances of humanity while making way for my personal truth to remain solid. While my mom was less able to reserve her judgment, my grandma let me exist where I was. She let go of her own desire for a certain outcome and joined me in my experience in a loving way. She showed me radical empathy. That hug stands out as a pivotal moment in my life—it was so transformative that it launched me on a journey of self-discovery and self-definition.

REIMAGINING BELIEF SYSTEMS

Although it wasn't a conscious thought, in the same moment that I signed my divorce papers, I also began to untangle myself from Christianity and the traditional expectations of a woman's place in society. It didn't happen all at once, of course. After two weeks of living back home with my mother, I found a job in data entry and rented a basement apartment in Akron from one of my uncles.

This was the first time in my life I was truly responsible for myself. Having left my mother's house to move to college, and from there into marriage, I hadn't ever really had a moment in adulthood to hold the reins of my own life. Not only did that mean that nobody was going to take care of me, but also that nobody could tell me what to do or how to think.

While the thought was intimidating in some ways, I released myself from the limited (and limiting) lens of Church expectations, fears, and truths my mother owned, and even from my former perceptions of my own abilities or interests. I didn't decide I was leaving the Church right away; I was just willing to step outside the lines of past expectations. This looked like meeting up with my girlfriends for a few glasses of wine at a lounge in the city (something that would have seemed scandalous when I was married to Manny) and reclaiming the sexual freedom my marriage had cut short.

Still, as a twenty-four-year-old divorcée, I was reentering the dating world feeling a bit unsettled. *How will I be perceived?* I wondered. On top of that, I had gained weight during my marriage, and for the first time in my life, my confidence in my body had plummeted. I now had extra flesh on my hips and belly, and tiny new rolls had begun to appear on my back. My arms were no longer as slender, and my thighs were touching more than ever. While I was married, I'd jokingly say there was more of me to love, but now that I was single, I just thought I was chubby. And I kept hearing Manny's voice in my head.

In the final months of our relationship, as we moved closer and closer to divorce, the strain of it had pushed Manny and me into more arguments, and more arguments meant more hurtful things being said to each other. Manny began to make negative comments about my body, pointing out how I had gained weight and how that made me less attractive in his eyes. So, by the time I decided to throw myself back into the dating game, I was feeling undesirable and not quite sure that men would find this new body I lived in as attractive as the one I had before I was taken "off the market."

Luckily, I didn't have to simmer in those feelings for very long. I hooked up with a former love who, after a night together, assured me that my body was still the body he wanted. We enjoyed ourselves, getting back in touch with the intimacy we'd once shared, and I walked away from that experience feeling back in touch with some of the parts of me I'd been clamoring for since leaving my husband.

For the next six months, I continued to get to know a Rachel untethered and unbound to anybody or anything. Everything felt like a new experience, and I took great pleasure in the most mundane things—like coming home after work and eating a burrito while watching *Scandal*. I reveled in the freedom that I could do whatever I wanted to without having to ask for anyone's input or permission. And given that what I really wanted to do more than anything else was to get out of Ohio and move to a bigger city, that's exactly what I did.

IN JANUARY 2013, I moved to Washington, D.C. As soon as I got there, I started expanding both my professional and social networks beyond other Christians.

This was fairly new to me, as I had attended a Catholic high school, socialized with my Christian community at college, and then slid into the role of Christian wife with Manny. But in D.C., I started meeting more and more "good people" who weren't Christians. It surprised me to connect with so many kind, loving people who weren't church folk, and I realized that my worldview as defined by Christianity had been quite limited. These new connections had meaningful careers, found powerful ways to serve their communities, and brought kindness and intention to our circles. To be honest, many of these people lived their lives more like Jesus than some of the people I knew from church.

This was a new experience for me. My concept of "good" and "bad" had been so narrowly defined by the Church that it was a revelation to have the option to show up to the world in a way that felt true even beyond the confines of Christianity. That's when I began to realize that I didn't have any interest in following the rules of a religion that felt much more rooted in fear than in freedom. I didn't want to be aligned with an institution that condemned those who sought a different path.

As I continued to meet more people who offered me a window into the nuance and beauty of something other than what I'd been prescribed by my Christian upbringing, I came to embrace the idea that I, too, could be a good person even if I didn't go to church. It was an internal dialogue that spanned a spectrum from grief—as I let go of such a potent and memorable aspect of my life up until that point—to a deep joy and celebration for what felt like an on-ramp to other powerful ways I could be in the driver's seat of my life experience. I gave myself permission to let go of Christianity, still holding on to the gifts that it had given me.

Untethered from religion, I experienced some hard moments as I wondered what my road map through the world might be without the Bible as my guidebook. Christianity was so convenient that way. How might I navigate the path that stretched out before me without the guardrails my church life had always provided? Between the Bible, the Ten Commandments, and ministers who claimed to know more than the rest of us, Christianity made it very easy to "stay on track." Stepping away from that required me to tune in to other sources of guidance life offered. This unfolded in ways that felt foreign and even, at times, untrue as I juggled what I'd always believed about the world with what was now becoming clear to me.

What I carried with me into this exploration was the lesson that *nothing is absolute.* I was again using my "keep the meat and throw out the bones" approach, this time to piece together a faith in a higher being with a faith *in myself* that would offer my heart and mind a path to healing. Luckily, I found the courage finally to listen to myself and, over time, to put my faith in my own inner knowing. I started to build a very strong trust in myself. Also, unlike when I was married to Manny, I started to pay attention to the ways my body communicated with me. Now when my body speaks, I listen. And as I set out on this journey to explore how I wanted to be in relationship to other people, I continued to integrate my rational mind, my heart's desires, and my own moral compass.

REFLECTIONS

IDENTIFY YOUR
HIGHEST VALUES

As I TRANSITIONED AWAY FROM USING CHRIS-tianity as my moral compass and leaned into developing an unwavering faith in myself, I realized that I had to determine my own moral code. This required me to identify what I valued in this life.

It was world-renowned psychologist Angela Duckworth, in her book *Grit: The Power of Passion and Perseverance*, who first introduced me to this idea. In one chapter, Duckworth lays out the research on resilience, clarity of purpose, and how to achieve goals over the long term. She discusses what she refers to as "core values" or "deepest values," the things specific to each person that spark and maintain that person's sense of passion and purpose. I highlighted that section of the book, and the wheels in my brain turned.

I was excited about identifying the specific values unique to *me* and my reimagining. This idea of core values felt especially powerful when I considered how ill-served I had been, and continued to be, as a Black woman by white society's values and even some Christian values.

I was especially intrigued by the idea of establishing a set of personal and intentional values to give me clarity around my choices and offer a framework to prioritize what was important to me. It felt exhila-rating and ripe with so many possibilities.

It also felt life-saving. I didn't realize it at the time, but living in accordance with my self-determined val-ues would amplify my work in ways that felt good—physically, emotionally, and spiritually.

IDENTIFYING MY
HIGHEST VALUES

..

So THE QUESTION BECAME: WHAT ARE MY CORE values—or highest values, as I began to call them? I started to take note of my daydreams as a way to map these values. I trusted that when my mind was at its most unencumbered, it would reveal these truths, this inner knowledge. Using my daydreams as a guide, I became extra aware of the content of my imaginings, like watching myself onstage from the audience's perspective. When I conjured up scenarios, what bubbled up? Where was I in those dreamy vignettes? What was I doing? Who was I with? And importantly, how did I *feel*? What was I yearning for in those moments when my imagination leapt forward to take me to a place that perhaps my current reality hadn't yet allowed or manifested?

During this period, I truly sat with the task not just of building a new life, but of curating a lifestyle and livelihood cradled by the things my heart most desired. All this was driven by a deep yearning for freedom—freedom for myself and my community to do whatever it was we craved without the constraints of an oppressive white gaze. Eventually, I landed on three truths, three values that resonated deep in my soul: ease, abundance, and opportunity. These were the recurring feelings, desires, and wellsprings from which I drew inspiration and that centered my life.

Having these values as filters was life-changing in many respects. The anxiety I used to feel about making decisions faded. Now I simply asked myself, *Does this action or choice connect to one of my highest values? Will it bring me ease or abundance or opportunity?*

I soon found that even when I was breaking a rule or going against a cultural "should," I felt confident in my choices and actions when I connected them to one of my highest values. Viewing my life through the lens of those values allowed me to give myself the grace to do the things I wanted to do and to skip the things I didn't. The only "should" for me became to have faith in and follow my highest values, even if that meant turning away from what was expected or deemed acceptable. I also found that I wasn't fretting over final decisions anymore. I had stopped putting myself through the analysis I used to torture myself with whenever I acted on something—the second-guessing. It's not that the decisions themselves were always easy or enjoyable, but because I had made them in alignment with one or more of my highest values, I now had nothing to regret. And if something didn't go exactly as planned, I didn't view it as a failure, but as an opportunity to grow my muscles and explore how my values played out in real time.

Part of the wonder and beauty of living in alignment with your highest values is in being able to forge new paths—as long as you are curious enough to step into that space. And because your highest values are not structures of meaning others have imposed on you, because your values reflect your own personal dreams and choices, you can trust that wherever they take you, you're right where you need to be.

ROAD MAP TO
YOUR RENAISSANCE:
IDENTIFYING YOUR HIGHEST VALUES

•••

WHILE I ARRIVED AT MY HIGHEST VALUES INTUI-
tively, you can use the following exercises. Activate
your imagination and use your daydreams and fantasies to identify yours.

Writing Prompt

EXERCISE 1:
Consider the Content
of Your Daydreams

WHEN YOUR ATTENTION WANDERS, WHAT COMES
to mind? These vignettes are clues to what's important to you. Be accepting of whatever comes up.

Write down what you see in your mind's eye. If
you're having a challenging time daydreaming, consider what might be keeping you from unleashing
your imagination. Whether it is fear of failure, regret,
or beliefs that have boxed you into holding certain
narrow expectations for yourself, allow yourself to
be critical of those things.

EXERCISE 2:

Meet Your Future Self

IMAGINE YOU ARE MEETING YOUR FUTURE SELF, whether she is five, ten, or twenty years older than you are now. You are as excited to meet her as she is to meet you, and there is no hierarchy here; you treat each other as equals. Where is she living or working? What do her surroundings look like? What is she doing when you arrive? Who is with her? What would your future self say to you? What would you say to your future self?

Journal about the conversation you've just had with your future self. What did you say to her? What did she say to you? Where did you two meet? Read over what you've just written and know that you are speaking to a part of yourself who knows, understands, and supports you. You are being introduced to your "higher being," someone from whom you can learn while still fully recognizing that the higher being is you. By sharing your thoughts and truths with your future self, you are essentially confirming for yourself that everything you need is within you. Then consider whether you've been trying to access feelings like these from outside yourself. How does that make you feel?

EXERCISE 3:

What Are Your Goals?

WE TEND TO THINK OF GOALS AS THINGS WE want to have or do—like "own a house at the beach" or "take a trip to Jamaica." But goals can also be how we want to *feel* and what we want to *be*. You may want to feel energized or be independent. You may want to feel secure or be untethered. These aspirations can help you determine how those desires might manifest for you.

For example, I sometimes wanted to feel the energy both of New York City and of my home state of Ohio. This desire has shown up for me as two homes, one in each locale—but my starting point wasn't "I want two homes." No, that end result flowed from my goal to have access to two places and two vibes, in alignment with my highest value of ease, abundance, and opportunity.

Write down the fifteen biggest goals you have for your creative life, your career, and your personal life. Jot down how you want to feel and exist, not just what you want to own, accomplish, or experience.

EXERCISE 4:
Whom Do You Admire?

WRITE DOWN THE NAMES OF FIVE PEOPLE you admire, and why you admire them. They can be people you know personally or folks you've learned of through reading or watching the news. What are the qualities or lifestyles they exhibit that thrill you? What is it about them you'd like to emulate? Next to their names, jot down what it is about them that makes them worthy of admiration.

NOW THAT YOU'VE COMPLETED THESE FOUR exercises, read through everything you've written. What themes or values come up again and again? Is there a pattern to your answers? Let's say you day-dream about buying a larger home that can accommodate visits from friends and extended family, or you've envisioned having off-the-hook dinner parties with neighbors and friends. Maybe you admire someone who is the consummate host or connector, and your future self basks in the joy of being surrounded by several generations of family. These may be strands of a highest value of "community" or "connectedness."

What are the themes you see emerging at the end

of doing the four exercises? These themes point you to your highest values. Reading through all you've written, what are your two to four highest values? Write them down in your journal or jot them down on a piece of paper and tuck it into your wallet. Start being mindful of using these highest values in every decision you make with your life, and then watch your life begin to catch up to your reimagining.

MAPPING YOUR
OWN MANIFESTO

..

Below is a paragraph from my manifesto
at the beginning of the book. I encourage you to use
my manifesto as a template to create your own. You
can begin by replacing the words in bold with your
own truths and leave it at that, or you can use my
words as a launching pad to construct a guiding
statement that feels both useful and meaningful to
you and your lived experience.

> My place in the world is sacred. No one knows
> me better than I know me. I honor and celebrate
> the ways my chosen self unfolds as I learn, grow,
> and shift. My beliefs are rooted in my trust that
> **my current self, younger self,** and **older self** are
> all partners on my path to well-being.

Whom do *you* trust to guide you on your path to
well-being? Yourself? A higher power? The ancestors? Replace your own guides, spiritual or otherwise, for the boldface words in the paragraph.

CHAPTER 2

REIMAGINING
RELATIONSHIPS

• • •

ONCE I OFFICIALLY MADE THE BREAK FROM THE
Church, I began to consider how deeply limited my view of
family and success was and how that impacted my concepts
of sexuality, romantic partnerships, and familial relationships.

Growing up, I had internalized so many messages telling
me that the most important pursuit is finding a romantic
partner and, eventually, raising children. But now I was ready
to reimagine my relationships in a way that made sense to
me—a way that better aligned with my truth, with the positive experiences I'd been having since leaving Manny. I now
had the freedom and space to investigate my sexuality and to
uncover my preferences for how I wanted to be in a relationship with future partners. At this point, I didn't yet know
what I wanted, but I was ready for the adventure of figuring
it all out. So, as I began to fill in the colors on the blank slate
of my new life, I dove into the dating game, excited and
hopeful about the types of people I might connect with.

In total, I spent three years in Washington, D.C., work-

ing different jobs and feeding my dream of becoming an entrepreneur. I also spent my years there dating different men
and learning about my own desires. I approached each relationship with an open mind and an eye of detached observation. Knowing I wasn't interested in a long-term commitment
with the men I was dating, I asked myself what parts of each
relationship felt good and nourishing and what parts made
me uncomfortable or left me cold?

There was Sahil, an incredibly sweet tech geek from Jai-
pur, India, who, upon learning that I had a particular love for
a good bottle of red wine, whisked me off to Napa, California, just a few weeks after we met.

There was also Lukeman, a tall, handsome Nigerian man
with a perfect smile, who worked at a bank not far from my
apartment. We'd sometimes meet up for a simple lunch on a
workday or take moonlit walks hand in hand past the monu-
ments downtown, sneaking kisses every so often.

Then there was Biko, a tall, slender Jamaican man who
smelled like shea butter. I'd come out to watch him play soccer on Thursday evenings, before we tucked ourselves away
at his place right outside the city to share a drink and laugh
through the night.

Overall, my dating experiences in the D.C. area re-
established my confidence in my ability to find joy in my
body and my sexuality. And by the time I moved to New
York City in 2016—in pursuit of a new dream, one that
centered my awakening ambitions with regard to entrepreneurship and community work and met my highest value of
opportunity—I was ready to further examine what connection, pleasure, and exploration of my sexuality looked like.

QUEER LOVE

HER NAME WAS VANESSA. WE'D MET ONLINE AFTER I DE-cided to set my dating app parameters to include women—out of both desire and curiosity—as I continued to uncover new layers of myself.

While I had always found women physically attractive, I had never given myself permission to imagine what a true emotional connection with another woman might look or feel like. It had been so frowned upon in my former religious circles that it seemed better to do away with any such curiosity. Though there *was* one time, the summer after my senior year of high school, when, at a party, I found myself incredibly attracted to a girl who had been dancing her way around the room. At some point, we were both outside, on the house's wraparound porch, red plastic beer cups in hand, while the music continued to seep out from behind the windows. I remember our somewhat hushed tones as we chatted softly with each other, trying to navigate the energy between us. I wish I could remember the conversation.

What I do remember is that, at one point, my hands touched her waist, and we both leaned in for a kiss. I was overwhelmed by how soft she was. Her lips, her tongue, the flesh under my hand. I was mesmerized by the contrast to the firmness men offered. She, this girl with whom I never even exchanged names, awakened something inside me that I then hushed for a very, very long time. But the episode made it clear that, while my feelings lay dormant for many years after that first kiss, I was definitely attracted to women.

So by the time Vanessa and I swiped right on each other, I felt ready to explore that attraction. I was flush with intrigue and anxieties that I finally felt free enough to investigate.

To this day, the thought of Vanessa's laugh makes me smile. For our first date, we met at a coffee shop in Park Slope, Brooklyn. As we both awkwardly sipped the barely touched cups of coffee sitting in front of us, the conversation began to flow with ease and excitement. Vanessa told me more about an upcoming show she had curated at a museum in Harlem. I loved seeing someone so impassioned about the work she was doing. I shared with her my "new to New York" stories and a few of my dreams for my time in the city. We laughed a lot. There was an unexpected amount of curiosity and chemistry between us.

Vanessa was smart and interesting, but I was unsure how to distinguish what we were doing. An often-lamented queer quandary asks, "Is this the beginning of a new friendship, or is this a date?" Fortunately, Vanessa soon made it clear that we were on a date. She was very forward with her intentions, for which I was grateful, because I needed someone to guide me through this process. This was just the first of the many ways she would hold my hand through my first romance with a woman.

Vanessa and I spent lots of time together over the next several months—learning about each other, exploring the city, listening to each other's concerns and celebrating the successes. We were enjoying ourselves in a very simple, gentle way that I hadn't yet experienced with a man. We were never inclined to fold into becoming an official couple, but there was obvious intention to the experiences we shared. We didn't seem to need an "end goal" to make the time we spent together worthwhile or meaningful.

Vanessa took me to my first gay bar, where she snapped photos of me dancing to "Dreamlover," by Mariah Carey, the song I'd pulled up on the jukebox. We spent snowy weekends in her third-floor brownstone apartment, where she guided me patiently through the rhythms and nuances of pleasuring a woman. We'd meet up for manicures some afternoons and call it a date. Some mornings, when I'd stayed overnight, she'd cook me breakfast, pointing out each item on the plate and sharing stories about the food from her childhood on the island of Puerto Rico. Our time together felt like a vortex of self-discovery, pleasure, and friendship.

But there was one thing: Vanessa had a boyfriend.

He lived in the Caribbean, on an island whose name I can no longer recall. By the time I met her, they'd been together for a while and were now in an open relationship. She shared this detail with me early on, and I quite surprised myself with how well I took it. My knee-jerk reaction was to feel manipulated, like she had cheated me out of something. But with all the groundbreaking discoveries I had been having around my baseline understanding of how the world worked, I allowed myself to get a bit more curious, to see how expansive this aspect of my life could be. I leaned in and started asking questions.

She explained to me how she and her boyfriend, in a long-distance relationship that wasn't always able to meet their needs or desires, had worked through what their boundaries would be, and they had been enjoying the benefits of the open relationship ever since. They wanted each other, but they also wanted each other to be happy when they were apart.

I was fresh out of my marriage and knew I wasn't running toward anything serious. Her unavailability for a long-term commitment aligned quite well with my lack of interest in one. And she always showed up to our shared space with respect, passion, openness, and consideration—many of the things my past monogamous relationships had tended to lack. I asked myself, *If my needs and desires are met and my values are upheld with Vanessa, what exactly am I fighting against?* Was my instinct to be offended actually rooted in offense, or was I simply grappling with the discomfort of newly blurred lines? Being with Vanessa represented one of my first opportunities to reimagine relationships.

Over time, Vanessa and her partner decided to close their relationship back up again, and I, though heartbroken at first, was comforted by the way they seemed to find joy in this new direction. I had learned so many things about the world and about myself while I was with Vanessa.

I'd opened myself up on dating apps to match with women, naïvely thinking it would just be a sexual experience, but after being with Vanessa, I joyfully realized the powerful romance and partnership I could have with women. This allowed a whole new arena of dating to unfold before me. My requirements for a lover began to widen exponentially from the "good Christian man" I was brought up to understand as the prize to a whole spectrum of human beings with whom to explore passion, romance, connection, and love. The world was gaining more color, more volume in my eyes. I was feeling incredibly grateful for this abundance that had been poured into my life.

The departure of Vanessa from my life left me with what felt like new puzzle pieces to possibility. I had a chance to form whatever picture of a relationship I wanted. I'd been given a glimpse into new frameworks for intimacy, ones that felt truer to my capacity, desires, and highest values. I derived so much freedom from this realization that I couldn't stay sad over the loss of Vanessa for long. She had essentially given me a blueprint for how I wanted to be in romantic relationships going forward. Now I could see a future where I didn't have to choose between men and women and where I didn't have to depend on one person to satisfy all my needs.

By stepping into my queerness and leaning into exploring what a framework of non-monogamy felt like, I was free to craft a romantic life of my own design. And when I asked myself what I really wanted, I came up with some clear personal truths.

First, I really respect and value the experience of falling in love, and I want to lean into it each time the opportunity comes my way. The bodily feeling of discovering chemistry with someone new, the intimacy of hearing them unfurl their story as you get to know each other, the friendship that develops from deeper connection. I decided that I want to fall in love as many times as I please in this lifetime. I want to be enamored with love's magic over and over, because for me it's one of the best parts of living. Falling in love offers the chance to be inspired in different ways by different people. It's the chance to discover new aspects of myself through new experiences. My interest and intrigue in someone would not be limited to a search for "Mr. or Mrs. Right" but, instead, a pursuit of those potent qualities of humanity that intimacy serves up.

Second, I am not averse to the effort required and the rewards that come from more attached long-term relationships. I began to read about and listen to how others had carved out their own containers of non-monogamy. While so many partnership configurations are possible, what felt most right to me was the idea of a primary partnership. Primary partnerships allow room for lovers on the playing field, but those other players must acknowledge and respect the boundaries in place with regard to one's primary partner—very similar to what Vanessa and her boyfriend had.

Third, I made a commitment to be as clear as possible, as early as possible, when engaging with people I have interest in. I must ensure that my own desires for fluidity in my romantic experiences do not cross anyone else's boundaries or conflict with their desires. This personal truth has shown up in really tough and exhilarating ways. At times, it has meant having to walk away from someone I was deeply interested in because monogamy was their preferred approach to love. Other times, it has meant being thrilled with the passion and rhythm of a relationship without having to constantly wonder, *Where is this going?* Sometimes the answer is that it's simply staying right there, in the soft, sweet space of attraction and exploration.

Ultimately, I made a commitment to relationships that represented expansion in my life. I wanted my experience with romance and connection to offer me space to feel soft and exploratory as opposed to rigid and finite. It's not just a place where I find pleasure but one where I ask questions; where I witness my growth; where I find inspiration; where I can both be and find a muse for creativity; where I explore different truths and various cultures; where I can appreciate different types of bodies, understand various perspectives, let different languages be whispered in my ear, and enjoy foods that speak to the heart of my lover.

Intimacy and connection are two of the sweetest things in life, and I look forward to continuing to find ways to cultivate them.

CHOSEN FAMILY

OPENING MYSELF UP TO THE MYRIAD INCARNATIONS OF romantic relationships launched me into thinking more critically about the limits I'd been imposing on myself with regard to *all* my personal relationships. I began examining how tradition, religion, societal norms, and even self-deprecation had built imaginary walls around how I chose to be in relationships with others. Emboldened by my initial experiences of freedom and exploration, I realized I could take the same approach to reshaping my friendships and their place in my life as well. As I moved away from centering marriage as the primary relationship in my life, I shifted toward a more expansive and critical definition of friendship.

My girlfriends near and far began to provide much of the stability and adventure I'd been raised to look for in a marriage. And as I considered their importance to my life, I realized that my friends provided more nourishment, encouragement, and love for the Rachel I was becoming than the family I had been born into, who weren't necessarily pleased with my life choices.

This may not sound groundbreaking—*of course friendships are a crucial part of our human experience*—but the intention with which I started to approach my friendships, an approach that approximated that of familial connection, was new to me. And it was so fulfilling. I realized then just how much my orientation in life had been toward finding a man and having children. But I was no longer on that traditional track, and therefore, my friends, I discovered, were no longer serving in traditional roles. They weren't just pit stops on my way to the destination of "Being Married." They *were* the destination—or, rather, they'd become vital companions on the journey to wherever each of us was headed.

With practiced intention, I started to build my *chosen family*, sharing with them everything from Friendsgiving to ski trips to important rites of passage. When a family member passed away, we'd all chip in to purchase flowers and be available in whatever ways were needed.

I met one of my dearest friends while working at a home-owners' association in Washington, D.C. An Italian woman much older than me, Mama Bert (as I called her) swiftly went from co-worker to stand-in mother. My own mother and grandmother were loving me from a distance, but Mama Bert's boots-on-the-ground support showed me that moms need not be blood relations. She fed me and supported me and was one of many older women throughout my life who became part of my chosen family.

Although my friends and I weren't all moving along the

same path, as a married couple likely would, the investment we made in one another's lives felt equivalent to the commitment I'd been taught could exist only in marriage. The diversity of our journeys—one friend was finishing her master's degree, another was navigating new motherhood, and I was pursuing entrepreneurship—and the support we offered each person's unique trajectory was our bond. I loved that we could all exist like that, works in progress pursuing our individual glories, feeding off one another's accomplishments, carrying one another's burdens, and experiencing one another's varied existences. It was freeing and nourishing.

One day, while listening to a podcast featuring Mia Birdsong, author of *How We Show Up*, I learned that the terms *friend* and *freedom* share the same Old High German root word, which implies a hopeful exploration of interdependence, how to build community, and what it means to belong. I loved that idea; it deeply resonated with me.

My friendships with Black women were particularly sacred and kept me (and continue to keep me) grounded through all my ups and downs. The Black women friends I made in D.C. and, later, when I moved to New York were and are my lifeblood. Clearly, I'm not the first Black woman to lean into her network of excellent sister-friends, but it can't be overstated how deeply comforting Black girl friendships are. There's a softness in my friendships with other Black women; a feeling of safety, comfort, and trust that Black women derive from being with one another; a shorthand of "existing while Black" that we slide into as easily as breathing. We don't have to explain to one another the exhaustion that comes with being "the only" at work; we needn't bring up the daily microaggressions or the questions about our hair. They get it. They know.

My choosing a family from among my friends hasn't divorced me entirely from my biological family in Ohio. My relationship with my nuclear family—my mom and my nieces and nephews—remains close. But I am estranged from my sisters for the most part, as an act of self-care. So these women I met over time *became* my sisters. They became the women I could count on for support, solidarity. They became the sisters my own sisters couldn't be for me—and once again, I was shown that I had the ability to choose.

This was what I wanted the relationships in my life to look like—chosen relationships (biologically or otherwise) that are intentional and mutually supportive. More important, they make sense to me.

CHILD-FREE

WHEN I LEFT OHIO, BURSTING WITH WIDE-EYED ENTHUsiasm about exploring the unknown and chasing my dreams of entrepreneurship, rest assured, babysitting was not on my list of avenues to success. But because I'd been watching other people's children since I was still a child myself, I was uniquely qualified to offer myself up as a sitter and then a nanny as I worked on establishing myself and exploring my entrepreneurial interests. Parents always need babysitters, and I was *really* good at it.

Once I landed in Washington, D.C., weekend babysitting was just another way to supplement my income at the mostly low-paying jobs I initially secured. But by the time I moved to New York City in 2016, my main source of income came from my being a nanny to the children of wealthy New Yorkers while I worked on building a business and engaging in my activism activities on the side.

Being in other people's homes for such large swaths of time, caring for and entertaining their children, gave me an immersive understanding of the day-to-days of parenting. More specifically, it gave me insight into whether raising children aligned with my goals and desires—a slow drip of self-questioning that took place over several years. I began interrogating which parts of motherhood I felt truly called to and which had been assigned to me by an influence out-side myself, such as the Church or social norms. I paid close attention to where I did and did not find joy in my relation-ships with children—and not just the kids I nannied. I also was more thoughtful with regard to the little ones among my friends and family members back home.

I quickly discovered that the things I loved about chil-dren were rarely those rooted in the "dirty work" of parent-ing. By dirty work, I mean the daily labor and inevitable inconveniences required of a parent during child rearing. The types of things that interrupt your sleep, skew your schedule, or direct all your efforts toward the needs and wants of one tiny human. Not only was all this utterly un-appealing to me, but it seemed to trigger something deeper than just my desire to sleep in late or have more quiet time for myself. It turns out that what made me good at nannying was the same thing that made me move away from the idea of becoming a parent: I had spent too much of my life in a caretaker role, caring for my mother and my sisters' children, when I was still young enough to need my own mothering.

A study put out in 2018 by the National Institute on Child Health, titled "Views of Teenage Children about the Effects of a Parent's Mobility Disability," speaks to my experience of growing up with a disabled parent. "Several participants reported feeling more mature than their peers or bearing more responsibility because of their parents' disability," the authors wrote. "Most notably when a parent has an ongoing progression of an existing disability or acute complications related to disability, youth may be at risk of feeling vulnerable . . . especially if they live with a single parent."

The effects of being born to a disabled parent were compounded for me when I supported my mother in raising her grandchildren and, again, when I chose an early career as a childcare provider: I was both highly skilled in *and* completely exhausted from caretaking. And so, I asked myself, *How much of my physical, mental, and emotional capacity do I have left to pour into another human in such a large way?* The answer was *Not enough.*

I also spent time talking to friends who weren't yet parents. The overwhelming majority seemed to feel not only certain, but particularly *determined* to have a child. They expressed their agony over eggs that needed to be frozen and their fantasies of small feet running around their living room. It dawned on me that I didn't possess a similar yearning. In fact, when considering how a new baby might fold into the life I was building, I felt more stress than excitement. I was surprised by what I uncovered during this time of questioning. I realized that when I thought about becoming a mother, my highest value, ease, felt threatened.

When I was a little girl lapping up Disney movies and being encouraged to play baby dolls with my friends, I was so convinced that motherhood would be a given on my journey. So these deeper considerations left me a bit staggered. My mind started to put the pieces together. Much of what I value—solitude, spontaneity, independence—would largely be suspended if I became a mom. Much of what I desired for my day-to-day was in conflict with having children. I enjoy slow, quiet mornings. I like long days and late nights for work and pleasure. I love a tidy house and neutral colors. All this doesn't actually scream "mom material."

But I didn't settle for just a "Cons" column. I also got thoughtful about the joys I found in children—like stoking their creativity by paying attention to what they naturally gravitated to, keeping them joyfully distracted while their caretakers took a break, helping them talk through the hard emotions their parents couldn't always attend to, and witnessing their personalities evolve like a miracle. My joy was found in ways traditionally seen as the role of the "village" one references when they say, "It takes a village to raise a child."

So, I began to explore other ways I might find deep purpose and joy in nurturing and being part of the villages I belonged to where children were being loved, raised, and celebrated. This exploration thrilled me. It cleared a path for me that felt true. It gave me space to stand firm in my own desires and remain child-free, yet also the opportunity to indulge in the beauty of family, connection, and intergenerational community. After much honest introspection and observation, I became comfortable with—and even excited by—the notion of being the person who pours her energy into *other people's* children, which I am able to do in great part because I have curated a lifestyle that allows me the time and energy to do so. I cherish the relationships I have with the children in my world, getting to be "Auntie Rachel." Motherhood is simply not for me.

At the time I made the decision to remain child-free, so much newness was already unfolding for me around my sexuality and my ideas of a relationship. The more I considered the fluidity of the life I was building, the more I realized that not only was a man not the singular option for romance and connection, but that kids weren't necessarily in the frame of my "vision of a perfect family." This idea wasn't always easy for me to sit with, but it was even harder for others.

Though there is certainly nothing wrong with not wanting to have children, society doesn't let you hold that truth with ease. Rarely would I get through answering the question "Are you planning to have children?" before the person who asked it cut me off to inform me that I'd change my mind when I found the right partner, or that I'd be missing out on the greatest love I'd ever get the chance to know.

Until fairly recently, it was socially acceptable for a woman to skip motherhood only if she was a nun, a widow, or was physically unable to have a child—and even then, she might have still sat with some shame for it. Yet, in recent years, more and more women have been delaying or opting out of parenthood. In 2018, according to the U.S. Census, nearly 50 percent of women in the United States between the ages of fifteen and forty-four had not given birth, the highest percentage since 1976—it wasn't until that year that they even started tracking this data. According to the Pew Research Center, nearly one in five U.S. women will end her childbearing years without ever bearing a child. Numbers are similar for women in the United Kingdom, where, according to a 2022 article in *The Guardian,* almost one in five women at age forty-five had remained child-free. Although, in the United States, white women are most likely to be child-free, the numbers of Black, Asian, and Hispanic women with no children are also on the rise. Their reasons for not having children are varied—including cost, the desire to remain independent, prioritizing a career, or not meeting the right partner to parent with.

I must mention that Black people often face an additional factor when deciding whether to have children. As a Black woman who grappled with the decision for several years, I considered what having a child would mean not only for my lifestyle, goals, and aspirations, but also for the child—I was deeply fearful of bringing a Black body into this world. My own understanding of the vulnerability and heaviness of existing in Black skin—how white supremacy insists that our lives don't matter, how there is no accountability when our lives are discarded, how I would have to parent a child in a way that included instructions on "how to survive whiteness and racism." None of us should have to add "fear of losing my child's life at the hands of the state" to the list of reasons to be child-free, but we do. Racism distorts every aspect of our lives.

RICH AUNTIE SUPREME
AND THE "OTHERMOTHER"

WHEN I STARTED LOOKING FOR A CHILD-FREE COMMUNITY online, I didn't find much on social media. A big part of me was craving a space where I could connect with others who had also chosen a child-free life. The few communities I was able to find seemed rooted in a very concerning rhetoric of disliking children or making fun of parents who had "made the wrong choice." I couldn't find anywhere that both wanted to shine a light on the upsides of our decision and find joy and excitement in being a part of the villages around us.

So I decided to start an online community myself. I called it Rich Auntie Supreme. The "Auntie" part is an homage to the "othermother" role, which, Black feminist and sociologist Patricia Hill Collins explains, refers to the strong tradition in African diasporic communities where women, blood-related or not (aunts, grandmothers, neighbors, best friends, teachers), step in as a maternal influence in body and spirit, as a physical presence and an emotional backbone. The "auntie," or othermother, role is an intentional and sacred one. Across time and space, othermothering has been a lifesaving aspect of our community—when mothers could not care for their own children, othermothers housed, fed, bathed, and loved them, ensuring their literal survival. Today, aunties and othermothers often take on an activist role, educating and supporting Black children and teens in a community effort to fortify them against a world of whiteness. Collins writes that community othermothering brings "people along . . . so that the vulnerable members of the Black community will be able to attain the self-reliance and independence essential for resistance."

The Black feminist heroes whose stories inspire and motivate me in every aspect of life were community othermothers, carrying (sometimes literally) their sisters and brothers in their fight for justice. And as sociologist Andrea S. Boyles, author of *You Can't Stop the Revolution,* has written, twenty-first-century othermothers, modern-day Harriet Tubmans, show up every day on the front lines, often (too often) in response to police brutality committed against, and state-sanctioned murders of, Black youth. They help to care for neighborhood children while their parents work two jobs, and they volunteer with after-school activities, regardless of whether they've borne a child. Othermothers and aunties do fun things, too, but the roles we have traditionally held are not the stuff of child's play.

The "Rich" and "Supreme" parts of my community's name signal that a child-free existence can be just that: supremely rich—rich with time, rest, spontaneity, and reward. The name points to a lifestyle that gives birth to joy, abundance, and possibility, rather than one lacking in some way just because we aren't mothers. After all, the decision is not to be whispered in shame, but to be lived out loud, with the same pride with which one expresses other big decisions, such as getting a new job or becoming engaged or . . . having a baby.

The response to the Rich Auntie Supreme community has been tremendous, and I've found deep delight and nourishment in the tens of thousands of women who make up our virtual village. Members of Rich Auntie Supreme share child-free benefits that boost their happiness—weekend mornings in their craft studio throwing clay, spontaneous vacations in the midst of a "school year," nurturing their inner child and spending loads of time on the crafts or careers they love. From investing in college funds to sewing pint-size Halloween costumes, the child-free lifestyle allows us to show up for friends, family, and even strangers with a joy and vibrancy that can only come from feeling solid in the decisions we've made for ourselves.

While I don't have any regrets about my choice to be child-free, it would be silly of me not to acknowledge the shadow side of it. Even I have had to work through the occasional bout of baby fever. The pull to procreate specifically comes during highly emotional moments in my life, like my mother's most recent cancer diagnosis or when I've fallen in love. But I've been through so many cycles of it that I need only pull out my reminders of why having a child wouldn't work for me, even in moments when it really feels like I want one. Of course, I have had to consider and plan for how I will be cared for in my old age, as I can't lean on my own children to arrange and manage that experience—a good example of why it is crucial to explore the shadow side of every big decision. Doing so is an important part of how I process my life, and it has proven to be a fortifying way to affirm the choices I've made for myself.

Being child-free has worked for me because the decision was based on what I value in the world—ease, abundance, and opportunity. Fully embracing my role as aunt and other-mother in the villages I am a part of feels true and right for me. My wish for everyone is that we give ourselves and one another permission to define our own role in the village. Parenting is only one way, but we can reimagine so many more.

THE CHOICE IS YOURS

THE FIRST SIGNIFICANT RELATIONSHIPS WE HUMANS HAVE in the world are hardly ever made with intention. We're born into a family and immediately become part of an intricate ancestral line of biological connections. Choice is not part of the equation. Parents, aunties, uncles, siblings, and cousins are predetermined by our DNA, with no real regard given to the type of person we want to become. When we are old enough to choose our romantic partners and how we believe we should participate as village members, too often we make these decisions—as I did—out of fear, tradition, and societal messaging that generally supports the status quo.

But we have the ability to do things differently. I've done it, and you can, too. We can all give ourselves permission to be ruthlessly intentional in creating our most intimate relationships. We can choose our family if the one we were born into doesn't value the essence of who we are. We can choose our romantic partners based on our own desires instead of society's limited precepts. We can choose how we want to show up as mothers, daughters, sisters, aunties, and friends.

Admittedly, when it comes to reimagining a "better version" of family, friends, or lovers, it can feel scary to go against expectation. But fear shouldn't stop you from having the type of relationships in your life you most need and desire. Yes, you may have to sit in uncomfortable resistance from others for a moment, and you may have to process the grief that comes with walking away from the familiar and from what feels safe. You may even have to be with the wrong person first in order to realize that choosing a life partner based on what society says is a "good catch" instead of what your spirit and soul cry out for will never make you happy.

And you must acknowledge that how you yearn to show up in this world might not always be celebrated and honored by the establishment, and that is okay because the only person who needs to celebrate your relationships is *you*. So, celebrate them, pour yourself into them, and honor them so that they can do the same for you.

There is so much joy to be derived from choosing who will be "our people," and a lot of frustration and resentment can be released when we no longer feel held fast to those who don't serve us. We shouldn't be expected to sit through toxic family gatherings simply because the people causing us pain share our DNA. Nor should we feel obligated to partner with a person of the opposite sex or of the same background simply because of historical precedent. We can do different if we so choose.

ROAD MAP TO
YOUR RENAISSANCE:
REIMAGINING RELATIONSHIPS

THE FAMILY IS INDEED THE FOUNDATION OF SOCIETY, but if that foundation is riddled with cracks of resentment and discomfort, then society might be screwed. We have to conquer our fear that redefining our relationships and self-selecting whom we honor as family will lead to condemnation of some sort.

In the African American tradition, we've been expansive in our definition of family ever since we were stolen and enslaved by this country. Our entire concept of family had to be rearranged to make space for fictive kin, family members created by circumstances—circumstances like slave owners selling children away from their mothers and husbands from their wives—rather than blood. Queer, immigrant, and other marginalized people have always had to join together to create family when they weren't accepted into what we have traditionally understood "family" to be. While history and humanity have proven to us time and time again that finding "our people" is a right we hold, we often feel constrained by the expectation to keep close to what has always been. But that doesn't have to be the case. We can move beyond the expected. We can reimagine our relationships in a way that works for us, honors our highest values, and nourishes our souls, regardless of what society tells us to emulate.

Consider the following journal prompts as you reimagine your relationships, both romantic and familial.

FIND JOY IN YOUR FAMILY. Believe that you are entitled to reimagine and create your own version of family, to exist in joyful relation to your chosen network and community in ways that nourish you and those you love. You are allowed to explore different versions of yourself, to step outside the traditional frameworks that whiteness has handed to you.

EXAMINE YOUR RELATIONSHIPS. Pour time and energy into the relationships that give you joy, and support and reexamine the ones that stifle you. Allow yourself the space to pursue different types of engagements and relationships, and note whether these interactions reacquaint you with a version of yourself you've been missing or introduce you to a version you haven't yet met.

BUILD A NETWORK OF LIKE-MINDED PEOPLE. Find ways to build a network of family, whether blood relations, friends, or a community of people who approach relationships in ways that align with your intentions.

MAPPING YOUR
OWN MANIFESTO

• •

I surround myself with people who affirm **safety, kindness,** and **joy.** I maintain boundaries that remind me and others of my needs and my desire to be well. I show up with my very best as a **daughter, lover, auntie, neighbor,** and **friend.**

What values do *you* need the people with whom you're in a relationship to uphold? Replace my values (in boldface in the paragraph) with your own. What are the relationships you most treasure, and how do you show up in those relationships? Mother, daughter, sister? Determine your own identity in your relationships and substitute it for my boldface text.

CHAPTER 3

REIMAGINING
FEMINISM

...

F EMINISM CAME LOUDLY MARCHING INTO MY WORLD through a television screen late one night in 2013. I was living in Washington, D.C., working days as an administrative assistant at a taxi company and weekends and nights as a babysitter, and female entrepreneurship was just beginning to pique my interest.

On this night, after the children I was babysitting had been tucked in, I flipped through the channels until I found my attention captured by archival footage of women marching through the streets carrying signs for reproductive and workplace rights. I sat mesmerized as the film unspooled information on the movement's leaders—in particular, Gloria Steinem and other powerful feminists who fought against patriarchal oppression.

I had never heard of Gloria Steinem, and I hadn't yet considered how the rights and opportunities of womanhood stacked up against those the men around me possessed. My knowledge of the women's movement was incredibly minimal then. But as I watched the dramatic story unfold, I real-

ized how misguided I'd been by my religious background to
think feminists were just angry women who'd been wronged
by a man or "simply lesbians," as my church often irrationally
suggested. Everything I thought I knew about feminism was
wrong. *So wrong.*

Although I couldn't say that I was a proud feminist after
one PBS special, I definitely changed my mind about one
thing: Feminists weren't the problem; they were leaders in
the march toward the type of world I'd rather live in.

In the months after watching that documentary, I started
reading about the feminist movement, and gender injustices
and how to overcome them.

I read about the milestone suffrage marches by the first-
wave feminists, in the late nineteenth century, and about the
fight for reproductive rights and equal job opportunities
during the second wave of feminism in the 1960s and '70s. In
the books I devoured, I met the anointed sheroes of both
movements: Elizabeth Cady Stanton, Susan B. Anthony, El-
eanor Roosevelt, Betty Friedan, and of course Gloria. With
all the heart and enthusiasm of a novice who has discovered
a new passion, I tried to learn everything I could about
women's fight for justice in America.

My entree into the study of feminism felt particularly
salient coupled with my research on women in business, and
the two interests nicely fed off each other, each granting the
other more importance for me.

Here's the thing, though: Everything I read about feminism back then had been written by white women, and there
was rarely a mention of Black women or any women of color
being a major part of the movement. The information I di-

gested was so whitewashed that I actually believed Black women had opted out of fighting for their own rights. I thought they'd bypassed participating in the women's movement to their own detriment. *Black women have got to step up,* I remember thinking as I took notes on all the advances white women in politics and business had achieved after demanding that their voices be heard.

The feminism I learned about by studying mainstream feminist texts offered a celebration of white women who were depicted as the champions of the movement and, without anyone to tell me differently, I accepted it as fact.

NEW YORK FEMINIST

By THE TIME I MOVED TO NEW YORK CITY IN 2015, I proudly claimed feminism and entrepreneurship as two major passions of mine. And New York City, with its fire-hose of fresh ideas, new experiences, and interesting people, had so much to offer a woman like me. A woman experiencing her own personal renaissance.

In addition to holding down multiple part-time jobs and collecting as many hours as I could as a nanny, I attended as many women-led entrepreneurial events as possible. In my mind, I had conflated the Girlboss movement (an internet influencer–fueled movement launched in 2014 that equated female empowerment with earned wealth and copious amounts of glitter) with twenty-first-century feminism. I believed that working hard toward owning my own business meant I was doing my part for women's equality and empowerment. Still, I knew I had much to learn about both feminism and entrepreneurship, and I was eager to find ways to do just that.

Not long after I arrived in New York, I decided to start a podcast, interviewing feminist women from whom I could learn and whose stories I wanted to share with listeners. The podcast, called *Proof,* was simple and streamlined. Each week, I'd release an interview with a woman who was going against the grain, doing things no one expected a woman to do, things she found challenging and meaningful. I wanted the podcast to offer young girls—like the one I had been, growing up in Ohio—proof that they could do anything they set their minds to.

My first guest was Dana Suchow, a body-positivity activist I'd followed on social media for some time. (If Dana's name sounds familiar, it's because you briefly met her in the introduction.) During that interview, Dana discussed women's warped understanding of their bodies because we've been socialized to see everything through a patriarchal lens. As I was still navigating my own relationship with my body and coming to terms with how much I did and didn't care about how I was perceived by others, Dana's words gave me much to think about. She also shared a lot of her own experience with disordered eating and societal pressures around beauty.

Our conversation was rich, and we really enjoyed the time we spent together, so Dana and I decided to keep in touch. A week or so after the interview, we met near Washington Square Park for coffee, followed by lunch a few days later. Soon, we were meeting up regularly and exploring New York together. Instant friends, we continued to talk and learn from each other about feminism, body image, and the unfair pressure society places on women and girls to be anything other than themselves.

One weekend, Dana told me she'd met some women who spoke about the work they were a part of at the Ms. Foundation for Women, in downtown Brooklyn. They were also members of the organization's Young Professionals Board, and they had invited Dana to come along to a meeting; she then invited me. There we found a wonderful community of passionate people, mostly women, of all ages who shared our zeal for political and social change. Dana and I eventually volunteered to be a part of the Young Professionals Board ourselves, and at meetings each month we discussed everything from pay equity to colorism from a feminist perspective, and we learned how to organize for change.

It didn't take long for feminism to become the center of my identity, informing nearly everything I did. My work, my personal relationships, even my family history—all felt realigned with my new understanding of how my gender impacted the way I moved through the world. Of course, I was disappointed that most of the women in the feminist spaces I was a part of were white, but race wasn't something I spent a lot of time thinking about then. Being Black was a source of pride, but I wasn't yet fully cognizant of how my Blackness—or others' whiteness—played a defining and divisive role in how the world of feminism worked.

That all changed in 2017.

THE WOMEN'S MARCH

Fᴜʟʟʏ ᴇɴʀᴀᴘᴛᴜʀᴇᴅ ʙʏ ᴀʟʟ ᴡᴇ ᴡᴇʀᴇ ʟᴇᴀʀɴɪɴɢ ᴛʜʀᴏᴜɢʜ the Ms. Foundation for Women, Dana and I leaned into our positions on the Young Professionals Board, committed to doing even more for the cause. I was moved by the many women who had made their way to the front lines of the feminist struggle and felt called to be even more involved in feminist activism. Dana felt the same way, and we were both determined to organize an event or some sort of activity to start making waves.

Donald Trump had just been elected president, so giving young women in our community a way to take a stand against the misogyny, racism, and xenophobia the Trump administration represented felt particularly necessary at that time. When the Women's March was announced, Dana and I decided that it was the perfect opportunity for us to plan our first event together.

Yes, the Women's March was already planned, but we decided to make an event out of the experience. We went all in and chartered a bus to support others who wanted to make it to Washington, D.C. With the support of our fellow Ms. Foundation Young Professional Board members, we hosted a sign-making party the night before the march. We reached out to feminist and body-positive brands for sponsorship and created goodie bags of fun and useful products, and anyone who purchased a ticket to join us received one. We were able to fill every seat on our bus with a dynamic mix of races, genders, and ages, everyone bursting with righteous anger over Trump's election. But even with the anger, when we arrived in D.C., there was still an air of hope and solidarity as we marched through the streets.

One of the women who had joined us for the march, and who helped Dana and me organize our event, offered to bring along her camera to document the experience. Her name was Kennedy Carroll. While most of Kennedy's shots were candid moments that captured the energy and emotion of the day, I had an idea for a photo inspired by some of the reading and research I'd been doing.

I had seen and adored the iconic 1970s photograph from *Esquire* magazine of Gloria Steinem and Dorothy Pitman Hughes, a white woman and a Black woman, holding their fists up in protest, and I suggested that Dana and I re-create the shot. So, we did. Even with nearly five hundred thousand people on the Mall that day, Kennedy managed to snap a clear, beautiful shot of Dana and me in front of the U.S. Capitol Building, holding our signs, unobstructed by others passing by.

The next morning, Dana and I both posted the photo on our respective Instagram feeds, excited to put the image out into the world as a representation of such a historic event. While Dana had a substantial social media following at the time, mine was insignificant. I hadn't had any interest in establishing myself as a leader or voice in the movement. I was simply happy to be in the mix, living out the values and beliefs I was now committed to. But with Dana's more than thirty thousand followers, the photo quickly went viral. People were picking it up and sharing it all over the place. Pretty soon, it got into the hands of the media and appeared in newspapers, on websites, and even on TV news outlets. That image and our messaging seemed to resonate widely.

With that photo out in the world, I was soon flooded with a large number of new followers on my social platforms. I went from having a couple thousand followers of mostly friends and acquaintances on Instagram to almost twenty thousand people now watching my feed. My Twitter account also saw a huge jump in new followers. And just like that, I was suddenly thrown into the conversation on feminism on the social media stage. Seemingly overnight, my face was everywhere, and news outlets came knocking, asking for my commentary on social issues, commissioning me for essays, and seeking quotes on what the photo meant to me and my feminism.

I didn't shy away from the opportunity to voice my opinions or recount my experiences; nor did I try to present myself as some kind of expert. Instead, I was honest about who I was and where I was in my own journey of learning about the movement and what twenty-first-century feminism meant. I didn't really care if people wanted to follow me on social media, but I continued to share what I was learning, and I did so in fun and creative ways.

This was what I had been using social media for all along—sharing what I was learning about feminism, entrepreneurship, art, and all the other things I loved about living in New York City—and I had no reason to change my online behavior. I wasn't interested in being an influencer or a professional content creator of any sort. I was learning out loud and building a community. Rather than be didactic with the information I was bringing to my page, I used my social platforms as spaces where I could invite this new community of followers to learn alongside me. I knew there was so much more for me to discover and understand.

By the time the excitement over the Women's March had died down, I was exhausted and yearned to get away for a while and regroup. Things weren't going so well with my entrepreneurial pursuits, and after all the wild energy of the March, I felt I needed to figure out my next steps. Dana and I continued to host live events for young feminists, and we had more in the pipeline that we'd dreamt up together for our community. I was also considering going back to college to finish my degree. So much was up in the air, so much was happening, but I felt that I needed to press Pause, get in touch with my true desires, and not get caught up in something just because it had given me my fifteen minutes of internet fame. This new Rachel who was evolving felt authentic but hurried, and I needed a moment to sit with it all. As we crack out of our old shells, our new surroundings can feel awe-inspiring yet overwhelming. I knew I needed to get away from the city and find a place to slow down and reflect on the journey I was on.

Luckily for me, I had a friend who was right around this time enjoying a digital nomad lifestyle with her husband, and she extended an invitation for me to visit them in Hawaii. I took stock of my situation and realized that, other than figuring out how to support myself financially while I was away, there was nothing truly holding me back from leaving New York City for a splinter of time. Sure, I'd gained a new community, but I trusted they'd be there upon my return and that I'd come back even better than I was before. I also knew that I might never again be in a position where I had the flexibility and freedom to take off for an extended period of time, so I told Dana I was going to hit the road and travel for a spell. We'd have to put all our projects on hold until I returned.

Once the decision was made, I quickly got busy finding a handful of clients I could work for remotely as a virtual assistant while on the road. I didn't know how long I was going to be gone or what I would accomplish, but I left myself open to the possibility of growth and learning.

THE WAKE-UP CALL

I WAS IN THE MIDDLE OF MY TRAVEL ADVENTURE—WHICH started in Hawaii and flowed into Puerto Rico and then Arizona—riding my bicycle through the streets of Phoenix, when the wake-up call you read about in the introduction occurred.

It was March 2017, and that photo of Dana and me at the Women's March had resurfaced on Afropunk's Instagram page. In the comments, I had been called out for being completely unaware of the white supremacy embedded in the feminist movement, historically and still today. Suddenly, I was confronted with big questions about a movement that had meant so much to me. Did I still want to be a part of it?

As I said earlier, I will forever be grateful that I happened to be traveling when this all went down. From Arizona, I flew to Japan for six weeks, followed by a stint in Thailand. In both countries, I spent weeks at a time in cities I'd never been to, sleeping in hostels and meeting strangers who were teaching me new things, getting lots of practice engaging with different ways of thinking and being—and my intellectual explorations of the women's movement felt like another part of the journey I was already on.

More than one person on the Afropunk page had written that the feminist movement was "never meant for me or other Black women." I asked myself, over and over again, *Is there a place for me in this community of activists?* Throughout the rest of my travels, I spent copious amounts of time looking into everything I could on racism and white supremacy within the feminist movement. I also tried to find resources on feminism that weren't whitewashed versions of the movement created by white scholars and thought leaders. From poetry to academic articles to YouTube lectures to open-access archives—I consumed everything I could. I even met fellow travelers who ended up teaching me things about America's racial history. I remember, one night, sitting on the floor of the living room of the hostel where I was staying in Tokyo, eating noodles with an eclectic group of people from all around the world who knew more about Black American civil rights heroes than I did. It was both a humbling and enlightening experience.

As I continued to travel, I kept reading, studying, and searching for any information that would help me orient myself as I grappled with who I was as an African American and how I understood myself as a feminist. As I made my way through Japan and then Thailand, staying at hostels in cities like Kyoto and Phuket, I arranged to volunteer my services in exchange for a room and sometimes a meal, and I often found myself working the front desk at the hostels—jobs that gave me the free time to continue to study the movement between welcoming arriving guests.

I was dismayed to learn of the racist attitudes and behaviors of the so-called first-wave feminist "sheroes" of the movement.

These white women acted in ways that stood in stark opposition to racial equality, making public statements that were the nineteenth-century equivalent of racist tweets. In response to being asked to support the Fifteenth Amendment (which, in 1869, would give Black men the right to vote), Susan B. Anthony said, "I will cut off this right arm of mine before I will ever work or demand the ballot for the Negro and not the woman." While campaigning for women's right to vote, Elizabeth Cady Stanton said, "If intelligence, justice and morality are to have precedence in the government, let the question of women be brought up first and that of the negro last." And I was sickened when I read that Carrie Chapman Catt, who in 1920 founded the League of Women Voters, said, "White supremacy shall be strengthened, not weakened by women's suffrage."

These were the women I'd been taught to look up to?

I was furious and felt blindsided. I now fully understood the disappointment felt by my Afropunk critics. These feminist leaders hadn't paved the way for Black women. Clearly, the only women they'd considered worth fighting for were the women who looked like them.

By the time I made it back to the United States after nearly five months on the road, I felt utterly betrayed by the feminist movement to which I had so sincerely given my heart. However, I felt I had no one but myself to blame for going along with the whitewashed story of feminism without question. But in that earlier period of my life, fresh out of my marriage and reentering the world anew, I'd clung to whatever felt empowering about the movement without questioning much else. Now I asked myself, *Why haven't I noticed the absence of women of color in the books I've been reading? Why haven't I looked around the feminist spaces I've found myself in and asked why there weren't more Black women there with me?*

I sat with the confusion and pain, investigating how I had fallen for it all. Feminism had been presented to me as a unifying cause with a "no women without all women" tagline, as a powerful and progressive shift from dated exclusionary mindsets. It had been sold to me as something *for* me. And not only had I bought it, but I'd *invested* in it. I'd been promoting and feeding a movement that, I was only now learning, had a history (and modern manifestations) of being harmful and dangerous in many ways to me and other Black women.

It was then that I experienced a profound personal awakening, and acknowledged the truth I had been blind to: There was an inseparable intersection of my race with my womanhood.

When I considered my wholehearted acceptance of this whitewashed version of female empowerment, I was embarrassed by my naïveté and angry that the movement had been dismissive of Black women for so very long. More than anger, actually, what I was experiencing was grief. I mourned the loss of the belief that I'd found a community and a cause that represented the greatest version of myself and that would support my growth and potential as a woman. That dream had now died, but I wanted to reimagine a new one.

But I wasn't willing to give up on feminism or the community of engaged and enraged women I had cultivated—both online and in real life—who seemed just as eager as I was to fight for equality and justice for all women. I recognized the difficulties, but I figured that if I was only now learning the truth about feminism, then the rest of my audience and community would want to know that truth, too. And even if they didn't want to, I needed them to come along on this journey with me, to redirect themselves away from the early misguided investments we'd made in the movement.

What's more, as a Black woman who had claimed a toehold of leadership in these very white feminist spaces, I felt a level of responsibility to share what I was learning. If I didn't, it would make me complicit in the very thing I was ready to fight against.

It is critical for us all to recognize the role that white supremacy and racism play in the fight for women's rights. It is necessary for us all to champion the Black women and other women of color who have been on the front lines of fighting for justice right alongside, and sometimes in front of, the white women who landed in our history books. I and many women in my community have a collective interest in making the twenty-first-century feminist movement an inclusive one that fights for the rights and freedoms of all women. I knew I was late to the party, but I could certainly get started

and join the breadth of Black voices fighting for our freedom.

That summer, I went from feeling betrayed and naïve to
feeling called to be an activist and a change maker within the
feminist movement. I decided I was going to talk about this
issue and keep talking about it until all my new feminist
friends and my social media community were on the same
page. While there was much work to be done to unpack the
racism within today's feminist movement, I knew the first
thing to tackle was people's awareness of feminism's trou-
bling past. If they weren't aware of it, they would be doomed
to repeat it. And the victims in that scenario would almost
always be Black women. Again.

My approach, as I took on my new mission, wasn't to
chastise or lecture people, seeing as how I myself had just
become privy to this information. Instead, I shared the information I was learning as I was learning it. And I was utterly transparent and vulnerable with my community about
what I was doing and why. In turn, I asked my community
to step up and commit to not being complacent. To prove
that they were willing to learn. And more important, I asked
that their activism be geared toward uplifting and supporting all women, not just white women.

I wrote the following explanation on my Instagram feed
in the summer of 2017, a few weeks after returning from my
travels:

> As I am learning and growing and finding my voice as
> someone willing to take up space as an activist, I ask
> that you be aware that I am pushing through barriers

that are sticky and uncomfortable and complicated and I am trying my best. I am fighting for my Black body, I am fighting for my humanity as a woman, I am reading and writing in search of answers that will lead to actions that will lead to some sort of sanity.

THE TRUTH HURTS

Armed with the revelation that what i'd been fed by mainstream, white-authored sources was cherry-picked at best and false at worst, I committed myself to studying the unflinching truth of Black writers, feminists, and activists—my intellectual ancestors, as I call them. I wanted to learn more about the contributions of Black women in the fight for women's equality.

It was then that I learned about women like Ida B. Wells, the pioneering journalist and anti-lynching activist who was forced to march at the back of her delegation during the first national suffrage march in 1913 in Washington, D.C. I got chills reading about how Wells, furious at this degrading request, initially refused to participate in the march. But she had a plan B: Defiant, she strategically waited in the crowd until her delegation had approached, and when they did, she took her place at the front, between two white supporters.

I also read about Frances Ellen Watkins Harper, an antislavery activist and founder of the American Woman Suffrage Association, who gave a famous speech at the mostly white Eleventh National Woman's Rights Convention, in New York City in 1866. Her speech, "We Are All Bound Up

Together," was a rousing call for unity that urged fellow attendees, including Stanton and Anthony, to embrace African American women in their fight for suffrage and that
exposed white suffragists for their hypocrisy: "You white
women speak here of rights, I speak of wrongs. . . . I tell you
that if there is any class of people who need to be lifted out
of their airy nothings and selfishness, it is the white women
of America." I realized that Harper could have given the
same speech today, given that the intersectional unity she
called for is still missing in our gender's ranks.

I hadn't heard of many of these Black female freedom
fighters until I picked up a title from a brilliant and kind
Black woman named Patricia, who sold books on the side-
walk in my neighborhood in Brooklyn. Sifting through her
collection was the highlight of many a Sunday morning for
me. I would walk up the cobblestone sidewalks of Eastern
Parkway in my Crown Heights neighborhood, stopping for
a coffee before beelining to her shelves and foldaway tables
outside the Brooklyn Museum, where she always set up
shop. Each week, Patricia and I would catch up as though we
hadn't seen each other for months, and she'd say, "Go ahead
and take all my Black history books, Rachel," knowing I'd be
foraging for more information on everything I was learning
and unlearning at the moment.

I struck gold one morning when I spotted a book titled
*Black Women in Nineteenth-Century American Life: Their
Words, Their Thoughts, Their Feelings,* edited by Ruth Bogin
and Bert J. Loewenberg. Flipping through it, I entered a
world populated by Black female heroines. My mind was
blown. In those pages was powerful writing by many coura-

geous and brilliant Black women of the past who had gone unsung in mainstream history books, women doing the work of abolitionism and women's rights alongside, and usually in the face of resistance from, the white supposed-icons of women's suffrage and feminism.

It was in that book that I first came across the incredible Dr. Anna Julia Cooper. Dr. Cooper believed that the education of Black women was key to the liberation of the race, an idea that was radical at the time. Born into slavery in 1858, Cooper was one of the first Black women in the country to earn a Ph.D., and at the age of sixty-seven! She lived to be 105, dying in 1964, just as the second wave of feminism was taking off.

Not surprisingly, I discovered that what I thought I knew about the *second* wave of feminism was also a whitewashed version of the truth. One that ignored the reality of Black women. Launched during the 1960s and '70s, feminism's official second wave wasn't the solidarity sisterhood I'd been sold. White feminists' pursuit of reproductive rights and well-paid professional careers towered over the needs of working-class Black women.

The second wave was ignited by Betty Friedan's bestselling 1963 book, *The Feminine Mystique*. In it, Friedan rails against the systemic sexism that relegated women to being only housewives and mothers. The book hit a nerve with middle-class white females, but Friedan never acknowledges in it that the rights these white, middle-class women were clamoring for—the opportunity to step outside the role of homemaker and search for more meaning and purpose in a career—came at the expense of women of color. The Black feminist theorist bell hooks lays this out clearly in her own book *Feminist Theory: From Margin to Center:*

> [Friedan] did not discuss who would be called in to take care of the children and maintain the home if more women like herself were freed from their house labor and given equal access with white men to the professions . . . She ignored the existence of all non-white women and poor white women. She did not tell readers whether it was more fulfilling to be a maid, a babysitter, a factory worker, a clerk or a prostitute than to be a leisure-class housewife. . . . When Friedan wrote *The Feminine Mystique,* more than one-third of all women were in the work force. Although many women longed to be housewives, only women with leisure time and money could actually shape their identities on the model of the feminine mystique.

The second wave's focus on equal pay applied only to sectors where the large majority of Black women weren't afforded the opportunity to work, being employed mostly as domestic help. Also, these white feminists' calls for reproductive rights made little mention of the medical racism harming Black women, such as the forced sterilization of the 1950s, '60s, and '70s—a practice that, into the 1970s, was legal in thirty-two states. Even today, we see forced sterilization being used in U.S. immigration detention centers and incarceration facilities.

What is plainly obvious in both the first and second waves of feminism is that the movement has never been one of solidarity. In fact, at no point in our country's history has there been a single movement that has fully embraced Black women and their issues.

After spending time revisiting the past, I started reading the work of more contemporary scholars, like Dr. Brittney Cooper's incredible book *Beyond Respectability: The Intellectual Thought of Race Women* and *Black Feminist Thought*, by Patricia Hill Collins. Studying these and other Black women activists who came before me validated my new sense of purpose. The truth about the feminist movement was out there, and I was going to do my part to share it widely.

With new intention, I doubled down on my role in fighting for equality for both my Blackness *and* my womanhood—and for all Black women. And interestingly, despite what one might have expected, the more I shared the ugly truth of the feminist movement, the larger my audience on social media, where I was cultivating my community, grew. By early 2018, my Instagram following was nearing eighty thousand.

Clearly, I wasn't the only one thirsty for this sort of unlearning and reimagining.

AS MY ONLINE COMMUNITY GREW, I realized that *what* I was fighting for had grown, too. It wasn't just feminism and women's issues. It couldn't be encapsulated in a hashtag. The conversation needed more nuance. What I was now talking about required looking into and understanding the components of racism, white supremacy, institutionalized racism, capitalism, sexism, and patriarchy. Just for starters.

This was what people meant when they brought up the term *intersectional.* And by "people," I mean scholars and activists like Kimberlé Crenshaw. It was this celebrated author and law professor who, in 1989, coined the term *intersectionality* to "describe how systems of oppression overlap to create distinct experiences for people with multiple identity categories." Crenshaw's work is often cited to explain the issue I was coming up against—namely, that fighting against sexism without fighting against racism wasn't going to help Black women and other women of color. Calling oneself a feminist without being staunchly anti-racist was doing only half the job. Being concerned with women's issues without being concerned with disability rights, income inequality, immigration policy, and the rights of the LGBTQ+ community wasn't going to move the needle toward progress.

While I suffer alongside other women of color and marginalized people who languish under the oppression of white supremacy and patriarchy, my focus, as I continued to teach, centered Black women. Taking my cue from the wisewomen of the Combahee River Collective (CRC), founded in the 1970s by a small but fierce group of Black feminists out of frustration with the white-centered feminist movement, I understood that by centering my fight on Black women's equality and freedom, all women would benefit. As the founders of the CRC stated it in their 1977 manifesto: "If Black women were free, it would mean that everyone else would have to be free since our freedom would necessitate the destruction of all the systems of oppression." Since Black women in America continue to be one of the most marginalized, vilified, and stereotyped groups in society, what was true in the 1970s (and before) remains true today. Knowing that I have followers in the UK and in Europe, I still felt comfortable centering Black women, because while our magic crosses borders, sadly so too does our marginalization.

The content I now shared online was no longer limited to women's issues and feminism. I began unpacking politics and current events—to the frustration of some of my followers, who argued with me in the comments without knowing enough facts or history to make a valid point. While I recognized the value of sharing information and engaging in meaningful dialogue with my growing audience, I did not see any value in allowing misinformation to be thrown around as fact. So, I decided to do something that might help us have more meaningful conversations.

Rather than personally rebut every erroneous comment made on my feed, I decided to offer up some simple materials of my own and curate a syllabus to study and learn from. I took time to research and find accessible and reliable resources on current issues in the news that people were up in arms about (human trafficking in Libya was the first issue I tackled), and I would compile the resources—articles, podcasts, videos—into one document and then make it available on my personal website. I took time to design each with compelling images and a smart layout to make it as user friendly as possible. I called the document a "social syllabus," and I encouraged my followers to read through the resources it contained before engaging in any conversation on my feed. I never claimed to be an expert; instead I thought of myself as a curator of information, and I suggested that we could all learn together. After the human trafficking social syllabus went over well, I produced another one, on the farmworker justice crisis in California.

The truth is many white women were happy and grateful to have these discussions with me and within the community. With unending displays of racial violence dominating the headlines—from the riots in Charlottesville, Virginia, to the multiple murders of unarmed Black women and men by law enforcement officials—they were justifiably angry and seeking instructions as to what they could do to be good allies. But they weren't always happy to hear what I had to say about white women's complicity in the very events they claimed to be horrified by. They weren't connecting the dots between police brutality against Black people *and* white supremacy *and* the patriarchy *and* their own role in all of it as white women. But I refused to be complicit in watering down the truth.

I would soon learn that many white women much preferred to ignore the truth. The more I engaged with my followers, the more I saw how little had changed since the early twentieth century. I was regularly confronted with comments from white women who claimed to be allies, but who struggled to acknowledge their complicity. I was constantly having to shut down "whataboutism" (holding up examples of successful marginalized people as a way to deny that marginalization exists, as in, "What about Oprah?") and their own "exceptionalism" (seeking to not be lumped into the conversation about oppressive systems because they viewed themselves as "woke," thus preventing the possibility that they needed to learn anything). Comments also suggested that putting a spotlight on injustices within the feminist movement was a disservice to all women's progression. In other words, I was asked not to air feminism's dirty laundry and to play nicely with others.

In response, I felt I needed to unpack white feminism in a streamlined way, so that white women could see for themselves how, historically, they have benefited from their whiteness and their womanhood and have utilized both to subjugate and oppress Black people, and Black women in particular. Moreover, I wanted to show them how this behavior and privilege continue today. I felt compelled to do more and to take the conversation further with my community.

UNPACKING WHITE FEMINISM

As I had done for other contentious issues, I created a social syllabus for the feminist movement, titled "Unpacking White Feminism," to help explain how and why white feminism was beyond problematic and mired in toxic white supremacy, and had been since its inception. To show, as I liked to put it, that white feminism was merely white supremacy in heels.

The posted syllabus earned mixed reactions from my online community. Responses varied. There was utter shock from those who, like me, had not been privy to the racism within the movement. There were feelings of affirmation from the women of color who were learning as well—finding validation in some of the underlying sentiments of exclusion they experienced in their own feminist circles. There were those who had already studied and understood this racist history who came to share even more resources we could continue to learn from.

Then there was the rage. As the post and social syllabus were shared more and more widely, many white women began seeing my work for the first time, and they didn't take kindly to being presented with a reality that demanded they be held accountable for both historical and current racial trauma.

The more I witnessed the resistance in the comments and in direct messages, the more I felt compelled to step out from behind my Instagram account and look these women in the eye, to engage with them directly, and to dig in deep with my time and my presence. I wanted to talk face-to-face with women like these, to see if real accountability and learning could be accomplished. To do this, I developed the "Unpacking White Feminism" lecture, which laid bare the whitewashing and racism of the movement, shone a light on the glories of Black women activists who fought for their gender and their race, and delineated the toxic behaviors that continue to thwart meaningful allyship today.

I gave the first lecture in Manhattan, to a group of forty-four attendees, with a livestream that welcomed any others who couldn't make it. I organized the event myself, hosting it at a community co-working space. Having recently done several events with Dana, I didn't shy away from speaking to a live audience. Plus, my presentation felt more like a community conversation than a formal academic lecture. Of course, I wasn't sure how this first audience would receive the content I was prepared to share, but I was committed to trying this in-person method of community learning.

And once I stood in front of that room and started talking, it felt like I never stopped.

BIRTHING KEA:
KNOWLEDGE, EMPATHY,
ACTION

OVER THE NEXT YEAR AND A HALF, I SHARED MY "UNPACK-ing White Feminism" lecture in more than thirteen cities. My followers from all over the country began to invite me into their communities and arrange for me to speak at their churches, yoga studios, co-working spaces, and, once, even in a beautiful quilting room. People soon began to refer to me as their first teacher on their own journey toward a truer feminism—a title I hold dear and have never taken for granted—which made me so proud and provided me with the motivation to continue my work.

Within a year of my hitting this grassroots lecture circuit, invitations started coming in from universities, racial justice organizations, and even some corporate institutions. It was no longer just my social media followers who wanted to hear what I had to say. I also began receiving invitations to differ-ent college campuses from both student groups and scholars. And that's how, in February 2019, I found myself on a train en route to Cambridge, Massachusetts, where I had been invited to lecture to a group of students at Harvard Univer-sity's Kennedy School of Government.

As the train sped along, I thought about how I could adapt my material for this particular audience, still marvel-ing at the journey that had brought me here, to the point where I was about to speak at an Ivy League university. It had been only a little over a year since I started my journey into examining feminism through an intersectional lens.

My public lectures and workshops were attended primarily by white women who were (mostly) receptive to, even hungry for, my unflinching perspective on what was required of them to "do the work" of anti-racist allyship, especially within the feminist movement. Black women also attended, looking to gain both a language and a framework for conversations they were having in their own worlds among co-workers, neighbors, and white family members and friends.

At the end of each lecture, I would invite Black women to come up and co-teach with me, asking, "Is there anything else I didn't say that you'd like to address?" This offered us all the opportunity to get into the nitty-gritty of more local issues. Often, audience members would call out how the local residents had been dismissive of things like public school diversity efforts, or how the Black community was feeling overpoliced at their housing complexes.

As the number of people seeking my insights rose, it became clear to me that these conversations were entering a particular cross-section of purpose for me. I was able to employ skills that flowed through me with ease: research, speaking, writing, and teaching. All these skills were braided into the very issues of feminism and race I was so on fire about. I felt I'd accepted a call from my ancestors, who had been sitting around quietly waiting for me to take up the work, work that had led me here.

On that train, on my way to speak to graduate students at an elite university, it was not lost on me that, until the 1970s, the school I was heading to admitted fewer than twelve Black undergraduates each year. I pulled out my lecture notes to go over them again as the snowy New England landscape rushed past my window.

Something was still missing.

I had spoken to many different audiences across the country, and it was now abundantly clear that it wasn't enough simply to share information on the racist history of the feminist movement. Spoon-feeding facts for an hour to a passive audience was not going to change hearts, minds, or laws and was also deeply out of touch with the way I wanted to teach. Engagement and action were paramount. It is not activism to simply post a black square on Instagram or to live-tweet about my lecture while continuing to participate in systems that oppress Black people. The change we needed required an ongoing practice; anti-racism isn't simply public acknowledgment.

What would their anti-racism look like, I wondered, *if Facebook and Instagram shut down?* But that line of thinking always led to contentions around intention. I'd repeatedly hear: "Many white folks' intentions are not racist, even if it comes across that way, and that should be taken into account." But there are very few instances where intent alone can carry the weight of an issue, especially not the matter of racism, where the impact is quite literally death. To hold intention over impact is to sidestep the real work, the only work that matters.

I'd also been contending with statements like "Black people aren't the only ones with difficulties. There are white people who are also poor or disadvantaged." This type of deflection from the very specific conversation at hand often discredits the role race plays in a Black person's lived experience. It implies that the world is an even playing field. For this reason, it was necessary for me to highlight that even a poor white person holds a space, a privilege, in that when they are out seeking social services, they are often prioritized over the poor Black person. Fighting for justice means ensuring that we are *all* cared for.

It was frustrating to have to spell out, again and again, what I thought was already painfully clear. And then there were those white women who were accepting of my uncompromising teaching but seemed to expect a simple checklist of anti-racist actions they could tick off in order to get themselves into a category of "Good White People," as opposed to committing themselves to this work for the long term. Committing to ensure the wellness and dignity of the Black people they claimed to be fighting for. The struggle for Black liberation doesn't end once white people have checked all the boxes of books to read, or lectures to attend, or donations to make. And it's not over once white people feel better about their individual role in the cause. Anti-racism isn't a self-help practice for white people. It's an ongoing process that demands a more critical way to exist in the world—one that dismantles the current corrupt system and establishes a reality that values equality and equity for all.

As the train hugged the coastline, speeding north through Connecticut, the wheels of my brain turned a little quicker, too—travel cues my mind to journey. White women already knew that racism existed in our country, even if some among their feminist ranks chose not to recognize it. I felt that for things to truly change for Black people, white people urgently needed to become intentional accomplices in eradicating what was killing us. They required a reality check to recognize that Black people have been doing this unrelenting work for centuries and that it was far past time for white people to put in the effort to transform the racist world *they* constructed and continue to benefit from. Marches, lectures, and social media shares were a start, but it had to go further.

I always contemplate the trajectory of any epiphany, including the one I experienced after the 2017 Women's March, when the Black community helped me wake up to the reality of a whitewashed feminist movement. What ingredients had been present for my awakening? First, I'd learned the facts. Then I'd considered how this knowledge affected my place in the world. Then I'd taken action to change the way I showed up in the world.

I jotted down three words I'd uttered casually thousands of times: *knowledge, empathy, action.* There they were, adjacent to one another on the page, strung together in a way that seemed to have weight. Once folks gained knowledge of the facts, the only way they really cared to take action, I reasoned, was if the issue affected them in some way, if they saw themselves in direct relation to it, if they felt that, unless things changed, they had something to lose. But in order to bring this about, I had to spark empathy—not the passive empathy of *I'm so sorry this is happening to you,* but a radical empathy that requires an examination of one's own role in another's pain: *I'm so sorry this is happening to you . . . and I will account for the ways in which I am a part of it and in which I benefit from my privilege in this system.* That kind of empathy has the power to trigger the concrete, meaningful actions that will directly improve Black lives.

Thinking of *knowledge, empathy,* and *action* as a set of elements essential for effective allyship offered me precise language and concepts that could help me explain to my audience what they could do after they left my lecture, and how they could continue the work moving forward. Staring at those three words in my notebook flipped a switch for me—not necessarily changing the path I was already on, but giving me a new way to communicate. Knowledge, empathy, action: KEA. With knowledge, empathy, and action, we move from the head to the heart to the feet.

As the train pulled into Boston's South Station terminal, I shut my notebook. I was excited about arriving at a new juncture in my understanding and teaching.

That evening, I tested out the KEA framework at Harvard and then continued to refine it until it became seamlessly embedded into the "Unpacking White Feminism" lecture. From then on, at each lecture, I demanded that the audience open themselves up to new knowledge, to unlearn and relearn the history of feminism. I required that they activate radical empathy to confront their complicity in the harsh, systemic ways whiteness shows up in the world and that they reimagine their role to be actively anti-racist in their feminism. Finally, whatever discomfort white women felt while attending my lectures or reading my posts, whatever defensiveness came up—I required that they sit with it and consider it in relation to the fear and outrage Black people have felt for centuries.

It's a process that anyone committed to being a true ally

for any marginalized community can engage in and use as a blueprint for authentic solidarity and, personally, to live a more authentic life aligned with one's values and goals.

MAYBE YOU MANIFESTED IT

FROM TIME TO TIME, I'LL POST A TRUTH FROM WRITER Corinna Rosella on my Instagram account: "Maybe you manifested it, maybe it's white privilege." Both a play on the old Maybelline ads as well as an urgent prompt for white people to consider deeply: How many instances in your life has your white privilege been the launching pad for, or "secret sauce" in, your advancement in the world? The post provokes followers to identify the moments when they may not have considered the ways their race gave them permission to exist easefully in a space that Black and Brown people had to fight to occupy. It also prompts them to consider the times when they *were* aware of their privilege but thought little of it because it was so socially acceptable.

It's easy to go along with "the way things are" when you're not the one being disadvantaged. You may naturally feel no imperative to change things, to reimagine the world. But it's these moments and these injustices, individually and compounded, playing out in every space that feed systems of oppression, that give "the way things are" power and legitimacy and further entrench racism in our society.

For every instance of white privilege there is an equal and opposite oppression of Black and Brown people. For every instance of privilege you experience as an able-bodied person or as a cisgender person, a person with disabilities or a trans or nonbinary person is stripped of their equality.

There's another truth I post on my accounts every so often, one I remind myself of when my intention is solidarity: If your only goal is to "break the glass ceiling," consider whom all those shards of glass will be falling on if you're not bringing the most marginalized people up with you.

The purpose of the KEA framework is to teach a simple maxim that underscores the truth of what I'm preaching: We exist in direct relation to others, and we must own the role we play in all spaces. That, my friends, is the feminism and solidarity we must reimagine.

WHITE FEMINIST ISLAND

I'VE LEARNED A LOT ABOUT FEMINISM SINCE I WATCHED that documentary on the women's movement all those years ago. Mainly, what I've learned is that the feminism that gets emblazoned on T-shirts and that is represented by pink pussy hats on the heads of white women isn't feminism at all. That version of feminism is what I like to call White Feminist Island. White women think it's paradise, but it's not.

A truer feminism lies off in the distance, but the waters between White Feminist Island and this more inclusive feminism are murky with hard truths and accountability that must be reckoned with. Over time, I've learned that, despite my many efforts to get white women to jump into those waters and swim, many are too afraid to go the distance. The more I pushed, cajoled, and demanded that white women recognize that their approach to feminism often wasn't safe for Black women and other women of color, the more they resisted and refused to look out in the distance and see that there was another space where *all* women could be free. They preferred to remain where they felt safe, on their very own feminist island. That's when I knew that if I stayed on that island with them, I would always be in danger of drowning. There's a line in the Langston Hughes poem "Freedom" that reads, "I do not need my freedom when I'm dead." That line deeply resonated with me as I contemplated the risk of dying on White Feminist Island.

It wasn't long before I began to burn out from the rigor of the conversations I was having with so many resistant white women. I was becoming weathered in both heart and mind as I tried to get white women to care enough to stand up for Black women, to put in the effort to ensure we were protected. After years of lecturing, speaking, providing workshops, and writing articles, I saw that the needle just wasn't moving. White feminists had made it clear that their race trumped our womanhood—that solidarity in maintaining the privilege of their whiteness was of more value than solidarity with all women.

I had to decide. I had to choose a front line, to reimagine my role within the feminist struggle: It would be either in convincing white women to care about Black women while waiting for whiteness to disintegrate or in being available to care for, nurture, and find joy in the Black community. In the course of this lifetime, I choose the latter.

I will always choose Black women.

ROAD MAP TO
YOUR RENAISSANCE:
REIMAGINING FEMINISM

My FEMINIST AWAKENING, AS DISORIENTING AND PAIN-
ful as it was, became the training ground I needed to reimagine solidarity writ large. Unearthing the facts of the women's
movement, and reimagining my place in it as a Black woman,
taught me to think critically about the world and offered me
the opportunity to develop the KEA framework, which has
become my blueprint for true allyship in any realm. My feminist epiphany taught me whom we should be listening to
and lobbying for and how those of us with privilege can support those who need systemic change, whether it's in the
area of poverty, class, gender, race, ability, or sexuality. Only
then will I practice real solidarity and be a part of intersectional feminism.

We can all reimagine our roles as activists through a more
critical consideration of the movements we choose to engage
in and by holding one another and ourselves accountable for
the privilege we hold (and sometimes wield) in the world.
We can reimagine these movements, and their potential for
change, by listening to voices from more marginalized groups
or to the people most affected by negative societal forces.

**Consider the following as you journey toward reimagining
your role in fighting injustice:**

SCOUR THE SYLLABUS. As you search for and consume
information to better understand a community, a cur-

rent polemic, or a historical event, be intentional in seeking out authentic information from reliable sources, teachers, and experts. Remind yourself that the most reliable version of the truth isn't always the one in the traditional canon or coming from the most well-known experts. We must reconsider what's good. It's not always the old white men sitting in their ivory towers. Try to find local experts, books written by people from the community you're interested in, and teachers who may not be affiliated with an Ivy League institution but whose lived experience makes them experts.

PAY ATTENTION TO YOUR PRIVILEGE. As the daughter of someone with a physical disability, I am hyper-aware of how the world is created for able-bodied people. I feel so much sympathy and anger for folks who have to live a smaller life because somebody couldn't take the time to install a simple ramp outside their establishment or a support bar near a toilet. Also, even people who think of themselves as marginalized and/or oppressed have privileges they may not recognize. Are you able-bodied, heterosexual, cisgendered, neurotypical, or food secure? If so, then you enjoy privileges that millions of people do not. When we recognize our own privilege, we become more available to empathize and then to act in ways that bring about change. What are *your* privileges?

DON'T GET CAUGHT UP IN CELEBRITY ACTIVISM. It is wonderful to see people with large public platforms doing good work, but we have to be careful not to "celebratize" activism. Too often, local activists doing major work in their communities are overlooked and undervalued because of so-called celebrity activists. We have to be mindful of who we are centering and celebrating with our time, energy, and resources. Is there a local activist you could be supporting or whose message you could amplify?

MAPPING YOUR
OWN MANIFESTO

· ·

I hold tight to my belief in **revolution.** Justice is not a passive pursuit but one that is braided into every way that I show up in the world. I name my privileges—**being educated, financially secure, neurotypical, able-bodied,** and **cisgendered**—and I use them as platforms to fight for the well-being of others.

Substitute the boldface words in the paragraph with your own belief system and privileges.

CHAPTER 4

REIMAGINING
EDUCATION

...

From a state school in Ohio to the Ivy League in New York City—my college experience has been quite varied, and my ideas about the role traditional education plays in validating a person's intellect and worth have changed dramatically. This journey I've been on—learning about myself, learning about the world, studying business, and unlearning everything I believed about feminism and race—has happened largely outside any classroom. This has been one of the most marked aspects of my reimagining: shifting away from a traditional understanding of education and, instead, leaning into practices such as community learning and self-study, ways of learning that not only have their roots in indigenous cultures around the globe but also that make the most sense for how I want to show up in the world.

However, getting here took much trial and error.

THE IVY LEAGUE

I DISCOVERED COLUMBIA UNIVERSITY ENTIRELY BY CHANCE a year after I arrived in New York City. It was early in 2016, and I had started working as a nanny for parents who required that I take one of their little girls to her Girl Scout troop meetings at Riverside Church, in Morningside Heights, every Wednesday afternoon. To get there, we always took the 1 train to 116th Street and crossed the intersection at Broadway where Barnard College and the main Columbia campus face each other—across-the-street siblings with reputations for exclusivity and prominence in the world of academia. Walking by this Ivy League institution week after week started to turn the wheels in my brain about what was possible for me.

I'd attended the University of Toledo to study social work right out of high school but left after my sophomore year, when I got married. A few years later, I spent just a semester taking classes at Wright State University in Dayton, but I chose to withdraw because I wasn't convinced that my major, early childhood education, was what I wanted to dedicate my life to. Older and slightly more settled now, I was eager to pursue higher education with clarity and intention. I'd been studying on my own, fueled by my interest in feminism and ethical entrepreneurship, but I was craving more structure, a way to tap into the things I didn't yet know to look for, and Columbia seemed like an exciting challenge. But could I, a two-time college dropout, budding activist, and amateur entrepreneur, get accepted into an Ivy League university?

One day, as we passed the Columbia campus on yet another Wednesday evening, I turned to the little girl and said, "I think I'm going to apply there. Do you think I can get in?" My young companion was totally uninterested and probably couldn't imagine her nanny as anything other than a nanny—not as a student or a teacher or a writer. But I saw all the wonderful possibilities for myself there—the courses I could take, the people I might meet, the skills I might gain. I knew that everything I was learning and doing on my own would only be fortified by the expertise and insight of the university's esteemed professors and by a cohort of intelligent classmates. Within a few weeks of first discovering Columbia University, I decided to work my courage muscle a bit and take the leap to apply.

After spending countless hours poring over all my options on the university's website and consulting with friends and mentors, I decided I would apply to the School of General Studies, Columbia's liberal arts college for students of nontraditional age or who have taken a break from their educational career. I was grateful that Columbia had such a program in place, one that would allow me to apply and begin taking classes outside the traditional academic calendar.

Once the decision was made, I threw extreme effort into willing this dream into existence. I pushed through all the steps required on the application: writing a personal statement essay, collecting recommendation letters from the most accomplished people in my network, and taking an entrance exam that weighed my knowledge and skills. On my application, I indicated that I wanted to major in anthropology, as it would allow me to pursue my varied social and cultural interests. After doing a bit of research, I was thrilled to discover that Zora Neale Hurston, the dynamic and prolific Black anthropologist and novelist, had attended Columbia's Barnard College in the 1920s. Her strong curiosity, the force of which fueled her work despite the many obstacles she faced as a Black woman writer and scholar, offered me a beautiful model for where my explorations might lead.

BY NOVEMBER 2016, the admissions decision from Columbia had been delivered. Seeing the email sitting there in my inbox, I felt my heartbeat quicken. I opened it: "Congratulations. You have been accepted to Columbia University." My start date was set for January 2017.

I was ecstatic. It was a moment of self-actualization, one that solidified for me that possibilities can become reality. One minute, I had been walking past the gates of Columbia University, and the next, I was glowing over an acceptance letter from them. Not only had it been worth it for me to daydream and reimagine something different from what I always understood as "enough," but I also possessed all the skills, the gumption, and a supportive community to push myself to new levels.

Upon learning of my acceptance, I started to map out how I might weave together my efforts to afford tuition, make time for classes, hold down my job as a nanny, and still continue my entrepreneurial and activist pursuits. It felt like a demanding prospect, but as I began to brainstorm how I might make it work, it dawned on me that my full schedule was nothing more than a list of all the things I absolutely *wanted* to be doing.

Toni Morrison was quoted as saying that her definition of freedom is choosing your responsibilities. "It's not having no responsibilities; it's choosing the ones you want." Well, these were the exact responsibilities I wanted. But I still needed more time to figure out how to make it all work financially—which at the time felt impossible. Just to hold my place at the school upon my acceptance, I had to put down five hundred dollars, money I absolutely didn't have. Sheepishly, I ended up asking the family I was nannying for if they'd be willing to front me the cash, and then take it out of subsequent paychecks so I could solidify my space at the school. They were so kind to say yes and, in a gesture of great generosity, simply gifted me the amount! But when I looked at the cost for Columbia's tuition and at my own limited savings, I made the decision to defer my entrance for one year, so I could apply for scholarships and arrange for financial aid. I wrote to the admissions department and told them that rather than begin my Columbia career in January 2017, I would begin in January 2018.

I think you remember what all transpired during that time.

Sometimes we think back and consider the alternate lives we would have had if we had shifted just one decision in life. That year between acceptance and entering the classrooms at Columbia would become one of the most defining periods of my life, and I'm so grateful I opened myself up to the option of deferment. It was during that year that I participated in my first organizing efforts by bringing that busload of fellow feminists to the Women's March in Washington. It was during that year that I took a shot at being a "digital nomad," hostel-hopping for five months by myself in cities all over the globe. But more important, it was during that year that I was publicly called out by the Black community to be much more critical of the feminist movement. It was during that year that I did a deep dive into learning everything I could about the whitewashing of the feminist movement. It was during that year that I began to learn out loud on my social media channels. It was during that year that I began to question the education I'd received over the course of my lifetime in predominantly white institutions. And it was during that year that my trust in many American systems began to wane.

THE TEACHER BECOMES THE STUDENT

ON MY FIRST DAY AT COLUMBIA, SPRING SEMESTER 2018, I joined a few hundred new enrollees for the School of General Studies orientation at the university's large, brick-laid inner courtyard with its manicured squares of grass. With applied credits from my time at the University of Toledo and Wright State, I entered the school with a junior-year standing.

As we wound our way through the hallowed buildings named after esteemed white men—Pulitzer, Havemeyer, Hamilton—our guide recounted the history of the university. When the tour arrived at Butler Library, housed in a building that looked like the Roman Pantheon, I felt added excitement. I love libraries and always feel most at home in their stacks. On my recent travels, I made a point of check-ing out the libraries in all the cities I visited, but it is the main library in downtown Akron, where my mother often took me as a child, that holds a special place in my heart.

Butler Library was grander than any library I'd ever set foot in. With its high, art-splashed ceilings, winding stair-ways, and the stacks of books in the building's inner silos, I couldn't help but feel inspired by all the information that lived there. I was stunned and completely delighted at the idea that I would have access to all those books and periodicals—material spanning four thousand years of thought.

As we followed the library guide, my mind buzzed with all the ways I'd be able to tap into these incredible resources. It felt like an inimitable opportunity to fill the gaps in my knowledge and expand my own teaching within the com munity I'd developed on social media. My ears pricked up when the library guide mentioned that we'd also have access to private librarians who would help us find information, not only all over the campus, but at other universities as well. All the Ivy League libraries are connected, he explained, so if Columbia doesn't have something, but Princeton or Brown does, you can have it mailed to you overnight.

I should have been elated. I was, actually. Private librari-ans? Whatever I needed mailed to me within hours? But then, of course, I considered the shadow side of that privi-lege: *If I have it, who doesn't?* Public libraries are, in theory, some of the most equitable delivery systems for knowledge I can think of. So, when I viewed the wild lack of access to Columbia's libraries for people who weren't Ivy League students through a lens of race, gender, and equity, it made it nearly impossible for me to ignore the injustice I found there.

In that moment, it was glaring and unsettling to see the number of resources and amount of knowledge that just that one university held with such exclusivity. The blatant privilege on display at Columbia blunted my bubbling enthusiasm. I couldn't believe how out of touch academic institutions were with the communities around them. That they would keep that much information behind a paywall. That there wasn't a direct connection between all the information they were gathering and the good it could do for people living in the neighborhoods surrounding these pristine institutions (and beyond). Hoarding knowledge is hoarding power.

That day, a gnawing feeling was planted in my gut around the exclusionary approach to knowledge within academia. While I was excited about what this access meant for my own knowledge journey, I was also pained at the thought of the many marginalized people excluded from this wealth of information. Behind these gates, behind these doors, and within these walls was knowledge that should have been accessible to everyone, not just a select few.

The same can be said for all forms of privatized education—from private preschools to exclusive college preparatory schools. Why are the wealthy prioritized for access to the best education? It doesn't have to be this way. In many European countries—Germany, Finland, and Norway, for example—public university tuition is free for residents and other EU nationals. The same is true for public universities in Mexico and many Central and South American countries, including Brazil. The belief system in these countries is that everyone deserves an education and that an educated populace makes for a better society. Tuition for college and even graduate education is subsidized by the governments of these nations. Imagine if higher education in the United States were a right instead of a privilege!

After the orientation at Columbia, I made two calls: the first, to my mother. I wanted to share with her how terribly anxious I was, how imposter syndrome was taking over my nervous system and how my heightened understanding of the way race played into the world was showing up even here, in my Columbia University orientation. I needed my mother's infallible ability to help me manage my emotions and stay focused on the task at hand. Even though she had no experience fighting first-day Ivy League jitters, she knew how to show up and act like she belonged in white spaces.

"Rachel," my mother counseled me over the phone. "You worked hard to get into that school, and they let you in. What that tells me is that you belong there."

"You're right," I said quietly from the dark corner of a stairwell where I'd snuck to make the call.

"You just go on and do what you have to do to get your degree. You know you're probably smarter than all those kids there, anyway."

The second call was to my friend EbonyJanice, a womanist scholar and author whose work toward the liberation of Black women constantly recalibrates my own pursuits in that area. I knew she would fully appreciate how elated I was to have access to all this information but she would also understand that I felt conflicted by my own privilege as a student there. I was constantly learning from EbonyJanice (and still am), and she lamented with me how heartbreakingly exclusive the access to resources truly was.

During that conversation, I resolved to share as much as I could with anyone who might need to jump the paywall. That's how my friends and I are: *Forget Netflix. Just give me your JSTOR password.*

Once classes started, I tried to immerse myself fully in student life, but certain questions kept swirling through my head—questions about the educational experience we Americans have codified and accepted as "the way":

Who determined which "core curriculum" would best serve me throughout my schooling, starting way back with elementary school?

Who determined which books were adopted into the curriculum my teachers lauded as representing "classics" and "the canon"?

Which journals were deemed worthy to be heralded as valid sources of shared information?

Who decided that Ivy League institutions—or four-year colleges, for that matter—were the highest standard by which someone could be deemed "educated"?

How does this system affect those who were marginalized, particularly Black and Brown people?

And how was I, as a student at one of the top private universities, contributing to or thwarting inequality?

The blinders had come off during my awakening to that intersection of my womanhood and Blackness, and I was beginning to look critically at every space I entered—and that included the university I'd so desperately wanted to get into. I refused to passively accept knowledge given to me without asking critical questions, even if this was the Ivy League. I was no longer willing to accept information without critically examining who was teaching it to me, what their agenda was, and what sources they were using to claim that knowledge as fact.

The thing was, as much as I was enjoying many of my classes, I was finding the university to be increasingly problematic. Another red flag revealed itself during my first week. A faculty dean was recounting the history of the university to some of us students when she extolled the virtues of what she considered the feather in its cap: "This campus still lives in the glory of 1893," she said.

This stopped me in my tracks. I side-eyed the white woman glowing with pride at the front of the lecture hall and then I looked at the two other Black people in the room, mouthing to them, "What the hell?" They appeared a bit uncomfortable, too. Could a dean be this tone-deaf? Did she not realize or care that, in 1893, a Black person wouldn't have been allowed even to *enroll* at Columbia. And when we were finally allowed to matriculate here, in the early 1920s, we would have been greeted with violent racism and bigotry. There had been an actual cross burning on the campus as recently as 1924!

Were we Black students supposed to feel comforted by the fact that Columbia was stuck in the glory days before Black people—or women, for that matter—were welcome here?

DESPITE MY GROWING AMBIVALENCE over the authority of exclusive educational institutions, I immersed myself in my experience at Columbia. I loved that I was acquiring more knowledge I could use toward teaching my expanding community of online followers and even just to shape my politics in the world.

I was drawn to classes that had an underlying criticism of various world structures—like Critical Approaches in Social and Cultural Theory and Gender and Sexuality in Africa. The conversations I was having with my teachers and fellow students were invigorating, and I was scoring high marks on my assignments.

One of my favorite courses was an introductory writing course taught by a brilliant young professor. Our goal was to learn different writing styles, including how to make persuasive arguments, which I was enthusiastic about, because I was being invited to write more and more articles and opinion pieces in major media outlets as an activist and feminist voice. Through my own research and unlearning, I'd been collecting many jewels of information on Black women, and I was primed to write about it all in this new academic way.

While that class was a place of joy for me, other experiences became constant reminders that I was a Black woman in an institution created for white people. One evening, while scrolling through my Instagram account after I made a particularly charged post speaking to the failings of American universities, including the one I was currently enrolled in, I found a private message from a fellow Columbia student. She wanted to let me know just how she felt about my criticizing the school she took so much pride in. From her picture, I could see she was white, and she identified herself as a current law student at the university. My heart fell into my stomach as I read her cruel and hostile message: She accused me of "stealing money" through affirmative action. She insisted that I was filling a diversity spot that could have gone to, in her mind, a smarter white person. She also suggested that I was profiting off the university, assuming I was on a diversity scholarship—which I wasn't.

I was paying my Columbia tuition out of my own pocket, cobbling together the money from speaking gigs, commissioned writing, and my continual work as a nanny for a wealthy family in Brooklyn. But even if I *had* been there on a diversity scholarship, it was clearly lost on this woman that affirmative action—in which a person's race, gender, or national origin may be considered as one factor in acceptance, scholarships, or hiring—has benefited *all* marginalized groups. In fact, according to many studies, *white women have seen more gains due to affirmative action than any other minority group*—more than Black or Brown people, and especially in the workplace.

By this time, I had almost grown accustomed to the racist comments I received via social media from random strangers, but this one had come from a fellow student. This was a member of the Columbia student body attacking me.

The predatory nature of her comment kicked me into self-preservation mode. The next day on campus, I was hyper-aware of those around me, questioning whether this woman's aggression online might manifest into something in real life. Not only did I feel vulnerable and angry on my own behalf, but I was fuming that this woman might soon be a practicing attorney, bringing her white supremacist ideology into the legal system. Situations like this one left me even more tender and more tuned in to the subtle ways academic environments signal that I and other students of color are merely an afterthought to the academic community.

Why would a fellow student feel okay sending such a comment if she didn't feel confident there would be no repercussions? Because there weren't any. Black students and students of color must continually deal with microaggressions, macroaggressions, and other racist behavior on predominantly white campuses because academic institutions in general haven't prioritized making campuses truly inclusive and safe for students of color. Increasing the diversity numbers is only the first step. Steps two and three should include creating policies that enforce consequences for racist behavior and designing courses and workshops for white students to address their biases—rather than lazily resorting to orientations for Black students to prepare them for learning in a potentially hostile white environment.

I DID SUCCESSFULLY MAKE it through my first semester, but not without the mind-twisting double consciousness of an elated learner and a frustrated Black woman trying to make her way through a white system.

As the fall semester rolled around, I shoved my misgivings over the racial climate on campus to the back of my mind and did my best to enjoy life as a student. I joined study groups and class discussions and attended events on campus during the week. Meanwhile, I continued to travel on the weekends to give my "Unpacking White Feminism" lecture. But my self-guided learning and unlearning had become so potent and, frankly, so enjoyable that I started to question if making Columbia work for me both financially and emotionally was worth all the effort.

Even before enrolling, I'd been having meaningful and challenging academic discussions with friends and scholars, and as a consequence of digging into the readings and lessons suggested by peers, I was already well on my way to fulfilling my personal learning goals. I would pore over footnotes and look up original source material, seeking further understanding via academic journals, documentaries, public lectures, and supplementary materials. I was already doing the work on my own that I was paying thousands of dollars to do at Columbia. And while I did enjoy the academic rigor of the classroom, I much preferred learning through my real-world experiences and with the guidance of the scholars and teachers I most trusted to learn from—who were overwhelmingly more Black and more female than the canon or the roster of professors Columbia was offering.

EXITING WHITE SPACES

ON APRIL 11, 2019, ALEXANDER MCNAB, A BLACK COLUMBIA senior, was walking to the Milstein Center library on the Barnard campus, which is open to all Columbia students, when a public safety officer asked him for his ID. He declined to show it, he later said, because as one of a small number of Black students at the school, he was frequently asked to prove he had a right to be in university spaces.

That night, McNab calmly kept walking in what he described as a "silent communicative act." He was barely inside the door of the library when six public safety officers surrounded him; two of them aggressively pinned him down. McNab then showed them his ID, and they finally let him go. But several other students filmed the incident, and the videos went viral, launching a university-wide crisis and an article in *The New York Times* about how students of color, and Black men in particular, were treated on college campuses.

By the time the incident made the news, I was in Atlanta giving an anti-racism lecture. I'd heard about what had happened to McNab through social media, but I'd avoided watching the videos—it was triggering to see yet another Black person violated at the hands and ego of law enforcement. But as I was standing in the hotel lounge, a news report about the event aired on the lounge TV. I couldn't avoid it any longer. A rock lodged itself in the pit of my stomach.

While I was grateful that people had been outraged enough to film the incident—undeniable proof that what Black students have been saying for years is in fact taking place—I had mixed feelings about that, too. The constant stream on television and online of videos showing Black people being shot, suffocated, and beaten by white people is its own form of oppression. Dubbed "trauma porn," it is reminiscent of the thousands of public lynchings of Black men and women in the decades after the Civil War (up until 1950), many of which drew crowds of white people, who treated each murder like a sporting event. Some spectators even held picnics beneath the swinging, lifeless Black bodies and had photographs taken and turned into postcards to commemorate the occasion. Black suffering and death are still a form of "edutainment" for the masses—but, in many cases, such "proof" doesn't move the needle on racial justice.

Watching this student plead for the public safety officers to take their hands off him, hearing him yell at them that he had every right to be there, I felt exhausted. But I also felt . . . clarity. For months I'd been trying to find good enough reasons to continue down a traditional path to a degree and teaching. But now I was confronting an undeniable reality: Even at one of America's most esteemed universities, one allegedly on the front lines of social change, Black students had to face the daily, ugly entitlement and oppression of white supremacy. In addition to carrying our course load and paying tuition, we also had to use our time and energy to defend psychological and physical attempts to strip us of our dignity, requiring us to prove, over and over, that we belonged in this space where a paltry 5.2 percent of the student body is Black or African American.

By the Monday after the incident, a petition condemning the racial profiling and use of force against Alexander McNab was circulated by the Columbia University Women of Color Pre-Law Society and signed by dozens of student organizations and faculty.

I waited for the Columbia administration to act. I held

my breath, instinctually knowing that in the university response would be the answer to my future on their campus. Later that day, the Columbia undergraduate deans sent an email to the student body issuing an apology for the incident and describing their shock. The remainder of the email read: "Our community offers many opportunities to take action, and we encourage you to connect with Multicultural Affairs and Multicultural and Social Justice Education Programs to engage further with these topics and the ways in which we can continue to improve the experiences of students from all communities."

I forced myself to read it again. Was the administration suggesting that it was *our* responsibility to take action here? Were they not holding themselves or the public safety officers involved accountable for ensuring the security and respect of Black students? Were they truly doing nothing to change their policy regarding policing so that this never happened again?

The president of Barnard issued a similar statement, vowing to review the safety officers' procedures and hosting a listening session for students to voice their concerns to the powers that be. Ultimately, five officers and their supervisors were placed on paid administrative leave—but it wasn't enough.

I wasn't surprised, and I was sure most campuses in the country had had some version of this incident and a similar administrative response, one that placed the responsibility for change on the very people being subjugated. Columbia's soft response was the opposite of the work I was trying to do out in the world. Presented with video evidence that people

they'd hired to protect the student body had inflicted physical and emotional pain on them, and hearing from a large
number of students of color that this had been their experience, what did the university do? They thrust the work back
onto the student body to figure out how "we all" can "be
better" in a tough world, thereby avoiding self-accounting or
any meaningful action.

In a flash of lucidity, I knew I had to take an action that
aligned with my values.

By this time, my Instagram community had grown sig-
nificantly. Hundreds of thousands of followers were now actively engaged with my unlearning and personal journey. I
wrote a post voicing my anger and pain and tagged the university administration. No longer in awe of the hallowed Ivy
League institution, I outlined actions I felt Columbia officials should take immediately—and should have had in place
already—to prevent future incidents of racism and hate
crimes:

- Demand that all white students and staff hold each
  other accountable for the racism they see;
- Outline a clear intolerance of and consequences
  for racism, and enforce those consequences;
- Provide financial and emotional support to Black
  students to counter the very obvious issues they
  have to deal with on campus. How are Black students supposed to exist and excel at this so-called
  stellar institution if we also have to bear the mentally and emotionally exhausting weight of "Will I
  have dignity here? Will my body be safe?"

Although my heart was incredibly heavy, my head was firing on all cylinders. I looked squarely at where I was, and I reimagined where I could be.

The Alexander McNab incident, coupled with all the ways the university seemed uninterested in supporting Black scholarship and its own Black community (Columbia's paltry acceptance rate of Black students; a dearth of courses offering Black perspectives; and a low rate of tenured minority professors, particularly Black professors, one that hasn't climbed above 4 percent over the last decade in the Faculty of Arts and Sciences and less so in other departments) compelled me to seriously weigh my options.

Should I drop out? Was that truly the best thing for me, a Black woman, enrolled in a respected program hoping to gain some footing in the world and perhaps even a Ph.D.? What if I couldn't succeed in my future goals without that degree? But if I stayed, how could I justify paying money—money I had earned imploring others to be actively anti-racist—to an institution that continued to prove that it wasn't up to the task?

Mainstream society dictated that formal education was the path to success, and here I was: I'd "made it." But now I was viewing it all through a completely new lens. I could now see a wider landscape of learning and how our culture stoked racism and other "isms" within the academy. I thought back to the many times over my life the system had denied me a well-rounded education, withholding the whole truth of my Black history, a truth that could have better oriented me away from whitewashed narratives of American ideas. I now understood with retrospective pain that what was offered up to me when I was a child—*read this, learn that, believe this*—had been curated by people who held little to no regard for what a smart, curious, strong Black girl needed and deserved in order to learn.

Academia presents knowledge to us in a way that suggests white people are the knowers and that everything and everyone else is to be known, explored, studied, and scrutinized under their white gaze. Even the books and workbooks my mother bought home to supplement my education tended to be materials she understood to be appropriate and good *because* they had been sanctioned or recommended by white educators. At every level of learning, the default belief is that the knowledge produced by white researchers, historians, and intellectuals holds the most value in the canon.

In the weeks after McNab's assault by campus police, I started reimagining what my future would look like if I left Columbia. Part of that process was to explore the shadow side of exiting traditional academia. I knew the pros: I could contour my education to learn both at my own pace and from the work and voices of people I trusted. I could take the money I was now spending on tuition and expensive textbooks and pour those funds into paying scholars more aligned with the type of learning I craved.

But what of the drawbacks? (I wanted to explore those fully, too, so I could give myself the tools to address any challenges that arose.) I worried about people not taking my teaching seriously if I didn't have a formal degree, and I feared missing the community of the classroom—the other students and teachers to network with.

To get help sorting through my options, I called several of my close friends and mentors, including my friend Krishna, a sweet, successful Black woman I'd met at an entrepreneurial event who quickly became a lifelong sister-friend. Could I become a successful academic outside the traditional educational system? I asked her. What could meaningful work as a "public academic" look like?

Krishna reminded me that I had the strength and where-withal to make it happen. She ran through all the possibilities of being an autodidact in today's world. We discussed what types of resources I hadn't yet tapped in to to facilitate my self-paced learning. She pointed out that I could spend my free time traveling to conferences and symposiums to connect with scholars from around the country and the world. And she pointed out that, frankly, I had already figured out how to engage in self-directed learning and teach what I had learned to a community of thousands of women through my lectures and my Instagram platform.

My friends also reminded me that the anti-racism work I'd already been doing was not backed by a degree issued by an institution, and it was already having a real-world impact. I wasn't hoarding my knowledge behind a pricey paywall, and I wasn't oppressing anyone with my own process of learning and teaching.

I spent time doing some real soul-searching, playing out the various scenarios in my head. What would it be like to prioritize my mental health, to give myself permission to stop living this double life of trying both to succeed in traditional academia and to urge my community members to educate themselves?

It would feel like freedom, I decided. I could be in charge of my own education, my own learning, and make it as creative and innovative and Black-centered as I wanted it to be. I could directly pay scholars I respected to consult on my writing and research. I could fund my travel to conferences and symposiums that would continue to introduce me to the brilliance of other scholars, passionate teachers, and insightful research. That all sounded ideal to me, the more I considered it.

And the more I considered it, the more I realized that making myself responsible for my own education was the same path taken by so many of my Black intellectual heroes. From Frederick Douglass to Malcolm X and from Benjamin Banneker to Phillis Wheatley, Black people have so often been denied access to educational institutions that they have had to take on the discipline and responsibility of educating themselves, even when it was against the law and the threat of death loomed large. Far beyond the simple image of an enslaved man teaching himself to read, Black thinkers, philosophers, scientists, and poets have embraced the role of autodidact and have dedicated themselves to ceaseless learning that led to life-changing advances in science, medicine, politics, and technology; brilliant works of literature, art, and music; and new dreams and definitions of freedom and liberation. Following their brilliant paths felt both inspiring and exciting.

And yet—throughout this process of consideration, I wasn't free of my own ingrained colonial biases: *Who am I,* I asked myself, *if I don't hold on to the opportunity to be affirmed by this celebrated institution?* I grappled with what I might be letting go of and losing out on. I questioned whether I would be worthy of respect as someone who had walked away from the ivory tower to explore a reimagined option.

I decided to test my decision against my highest values of ease, abundance, and opportunity. Walking away from an Ivy League education might, on the face of it, look like walking away from an *opportunity,* but I saw it as the opposite. Granting myself permission to chart my own path of learning would open up a world of new opportunities with regard to where, how, and with whom I could learn. Also, when I compared the *ease* with which I was able to take in knowledge when it had been arranged by my own hand with the mental gymnastics I had to perform on the Columbia campus just to feel safe, supported, and unbothered by the privilege on display there, there was no comparison. And despite the four thousand years of knowledge stashed inside the walls of Butler Library, it was obvious to me that the *abundance* of knowledge I had access to outside Columbia's matrix was itself immense.

Using my highest values as the crux of consideration felt useful to get me to the other side of making the decision, but it still required courage to walk away from something that had once held so much weight in my vision of my future self. Yet, I couldn't ignore the feeling in my gut. Just as I'd learned during my divorce, my body offers valuable signals, too. Its clenching was its way of urging me to trust myself and heed my own instincts. My gut knew that Columbia wasn't the place for me. And so, I made a decision that felt right to me, not caring if it didn't sit right with others.

Before the new semester arrived, I withdrew from Columbia. In total, I had spent one year as an enrolled student there. Any fear I harbored was quickly replaced with a rush of excitement and curiosity over what lay ahead. Even though I didn't have the certainty of a degree track or an alma mater behind my efforts, I trusted that making this decision based on my highest values and needs would fortify me enough to take the leap. I knew that my next step, my next action, my next reimagining, would be truthful and liberating.

I was excited about what awaited me outside the classroom and the gates of this stuck-in-1893 university. I was nervous but thrilled to be able to reimagine everything I thought I knew about education, to learn from people of color, and to honor the work of Black intellectuals and other marginalized voices, whether they were affiliated with a university or not.

Here's what I wrote to my online community shortly after leaving Columbia:

> My decision to leave Columbia is not an easy one. I acknowledge my privilege of having the opportunity to attend an institution that holds so much prestige in our society. But I have decided that now I must use my platform to address the ways that something as meaningful as education is quite often harming the very people who pursue it.

I can no longer stomach handing over thousands of dollars to an institution that continues to brush aside the blatant discrimination happening on its campus. Each major moment of heartbreaking racism that has happened on Columbia's campus as of late has been met, not with responsibility and action, but instead with vague acknowledgment and minimal accountability.

While I considered other institutions, I have made the final decision to pursue independent study outside of enrollment to any particular campus or college.

I am terrified, I am hopeful, I am determined.

Here is how I am doing it:

1. I am working one on one with scholars whose work I learn from and respect. Together we are building a unique curriculum that addresses my learning goals.
2. I am taking occasional individual courses at various institutions such as Brooklyn Institute of Social Research and others like it where I can engage in critical classroom conversation.
3. I am pursuing various fellowships and residencies to continue to build on my writing and research skills.
4. I am opening my mind and heart to what other ways I can show up in scholarship and in the pursuit of knowledge that I so deeply crave to obtain and teach as I continue on in this journey.

AUTODIDACT

IN THE SPRING OF 2019, AS I OFFICIALLY EMBARKED ON MY journey as an independent scholar, I knew where I wanted my learning centered: on Blackness and womanhood. An opportunity for me to do a deep dive into the very things that make up who I am and that need continued efforts from all of us in order for us to move toward freedom and justice. I took my time to research spaces that taught in a way I desired to learn. I enrolled in classes at small, independent organizations that offered community teaching. I registered for and attended lectures offered by public institutions around the city, such as the Schomburg Center for Research in Black Culture. I enrolled in one-off night courses for adults at various spaces around New York City, such as History of Black Theater at Juilliard. I also independently registered and attended social and academic conferences such as the Black Girls Equity Alliance Equity Summit. I humbly reached out to professors I admired and requested access to the syllabuses they used in their classes, and I read the books and articles they assigned. I sat with mentors and other peers to share writing and debate stances, to get feedback on what and how I was understanding things.

It was invigorating and empowering to be in charge of my own learning, and I couldn't help but feel the shift in excitement within my body. Everything I was consuming would benefit the work I was doing both as a public academic and in building my enterprises.

The synergy of my work inspiring my learning and my learning feeding my work has left me with a sense of utter satisfaction and has given me clear confirmation that I made the right decision in walking away from Columbia. Even when I come across the odd inquisitor who challenges my right to teach, or the random critic of the choices I've made, I have no regrets. The indescribable sense of purpose that fuels me every day as I continue to teach, speak, and learn is indeed, for me, enough.

EDUCATION VS. KNOWLEDGE

SINCE LEAVING COLUMBIA AND EMBRACING MY IDENTITY as an autodidact, I've come to replace my value for education with a deeper value for knowledge. Education is associated with schools and universities, but knowledge lives beyond the walls of an institution.

As a person with unceasing curiosity and an unlimited desire to continue studying and learning about the subjects important to my work and my passions, I now feel confident saying I am constantly looking for ways to increase my knowledge as opposed to "get a good education." I have come to the point in my life where I can fully trust in my own abilities to gather the knowledge I need. The fact of the matter is that we now live in a world where knowledge is more accessible than ever.

I would be remiss if I didn't give a shout-out to public libraries, all across the United States and globally, which are having a renaissance of their own, reimagining themselves not only as repositories for books and printed materials, but also as co-working spaces, healthcare centers, activist hubs, and even cooking schools—that is, repositories of information writ large. In other words, whatever you want to increase your knowledge in, odds are that information is available for the taking at a public library.

I have also made peace with myself regarding the need for a title conferred by an institution of higher learning. I've known since I was a little girl that education doesn't require a classroom, but I still had to reimagine what "self-education" would look like for me and what it would sound like coming out of the mouths of others. After all, whereas I may call myself a public academic, a stranger or critic might brand me a three-time college dropout. But as my mother always reminds me, "You can't build your truth on what other people think."

My decision to embrace self-learning was based not only on what felt good and right to me but also on my style of learning and how I wanted to experience the world. As a lecturer, writer, and entrepreneur, I feel it incumbent upon me to lean into a deeper understanding of the world around me, both its historic and present-day truths. And because I've taken on the role of autodidact as a lifetime journey, I consider knowledge as being on a continuum rather than as a destination.

When I look at what has happened in my career and my life since I decided to leave Columbia, all I see is the success I always craved and the renaissance I imagined for myself.

ROAD MAP TO
YOUR RENAISSANCE:
REIMAGINING LEARNING

I**T IS INTERESTING TO ME THAT WE HAVE SEEN A RISE IN** the number of homeschoolers in the United States, particularly among African American families. Not too long ago, homeschooling was considered taboo or something appropriate only for child stars or religious extremists. But these days, Black people in particular are turning to homeschooling because they have critically assessed the educational options for their children in their cities and neighborhoods and decided that what they are being taught doesn't serve them. Moreover, much of what is being taught is from curriculums steeped in white supremacy.

Globally, we are also seeing a rise in something called world schooling, or unschooling, where parents take a child-led approach to educating their little ones, and the entire world becomes a classroom, with learning driven mainly by the child's natural curiosity. In other words, people all over the world are reimagining what education and learning look like.

But the freedom to do so shouldn't be relegated to children. As adults, we should all commit to a lifetime journey of learning. Education must not be associated only with schools, and learning should not require the rigid structure of traditional academic institutions. The sooner we acknowledge that we have the power and the access to learn without gatekeepers, the freer we will become to reimagine a reality for ourselves that aligns with our values, passions, and goals. Does this mean we should eschew all traditional educational models? Should doctors skip medical school? Do we want engineers to make up their own laws of physics? Absolutely not. A distinction should be made between the training a person must complete to learn a specific craft, science, or skill and the learning and knowledge-gathering all of us must do as human beings.

My wish is to inspire you to consider the multitude of ways you can increase your knowledge and continue to learn throughout your lifetime. My hope is that you see opportunities everywhere to learn and grow—in books written by New Age healers, in workshops taught in the basement of a church, on excursions out into the wilderness led by an elder. Maybe that excursion will make you a better doctor. Maybe that workshop will lead you to a new career. The goal is not the destination, however. The goal is the journey and where it takes you.

Consider the following as you reimagine what your approach to knowledge and learning might look like:

ENVISION THE WORLD AS YOUR CLASSROOM. Take a cue from the world school community and disavow the notion that the only place you learn new things is within a designed curriculum. Begin the process of seeing opportunities to learn everywhere you go, whether it's a library, a museum, or the grocery store. Fun fact: Anthropologists often spend time in grocery stores to learn about the eating habits and culture of local populations.

REIGNITE YOUR LEARNING MUSCLE. For many people, the monotony of everyday life puts the learning muscle to sleep, and they forget how to lean into new things. Sign up for a class, even if it's a one-day workshop on flower arranging. Get your learning muscle back in shape and choose a topic you're genuinely interested in, to remind yourself that learning is fun.

AMAZE YOURSELF WITH THE POSSIBILITIES. Start a running list of all the resources in your world for continued learning: where you might take a class, attend a lecture, learn a new skill. Open yourself to all the opportunities available to you to continue learning without officially going back to school.

VISIT A PUBLIC LIBRARY. Just go and see.

MAPPING YOUR
OWN MANIFESTO

· ·

It is an honor to learn my way through this lifetime. I commit myself to my curiosity and interests. Gaining new and deeper knowledge not
only of myself but also of **art** and **the history of
Black feminism** is always a worthy use of my
time.

Replace the words in boldface in the paragraph
from my manifesto with what *you* are committed to
learning about throughout *your* lifetime.

CHAPTER 5

REIMAGINING WORK

...

As a child, I had a more straightforward vision of my professional future than where I stand today. I imagine we all did. Back then, I wanted to be a teacher. I'd stand in my makeshift classroom, facing a row of dolls and stuffed animals, teaching the lessons I'd created. Sometimes, I would force my little sister Myriah to play one of my students, so I could have a real person to instruct.

I remember sitting at my mom's dining room table diligently creating worksheets that mimicked the ones I was completing in my elementary school classes at the time. (I loved making worksheets!) With my colored pencils, crayons, and markers, I'd write down questions accompanied by perfect little checkboxes for the answers. I also loved coming up with lesson plans and writing them down in my spiral notebook. To me, preparing the lesson was the best part of the job.

It isn't lost on me that, today, at the core of all of the work that I do, I am a teacher. Whether I'm writing, lecturing, curating on social media, or creating an actual syllabus, I am a teacher. Even my entrepreneurial pursuits have given me the opportunity to instruct others in ways they, too, can build a business that fits their purpose, dreams, and goals. It is deeply satisfying to know that teaching is the core of the world I have created for myself, not only because I enjoy the work, but because it feels like a teacher is who I was meant to be. I have stepped into a purpose that has been familiar to me since I was a child.

The business I've built around that teaching feels equally purposeful. I've found that, for many of us, there are hints and clues in where we found joy as a child that reflect heavily the joy we find as adults. Sometimes that earlier joy braids seamlessly into the career we choose; other times, it is where we find our grounding in day-to-day life. I am a firm believer that our younger selves can offer insights into what will make us whole as adults. My best advice to you is that it is never too late to find and live the truth your younger self has to offer.

It was in my early days in Washington, D.C., that I got the inkling that aside from teaching there was another major part of my approach to work—entrepreneurship. I was beginning to feel drawn to the idea that my life's work would ideally involve me building out something of my own. What started as a simple whisper—listening to those podcasts and watching those TED Talks as a housewife—became a louder urging as I explored what was possible. When I dove into the Girlboss movement unfurling in real time as I was looking for a path for my nascent entrepreneurial desires, I felt empowered and excited. The calling was hazy then, yet I knew, as I kept researching, learning new skills, and asking questions, that a life and career I both chose myself and truly loved could take shape. We often expect that "the dream" will come to us with an architect's blueprints for how to build it, but sometimes it's just a seed. While I didn't yet see the full picture of what I could build out, what I did have were my values, my courage, and the deep desire to reimagine entrepreneurship in a way that worked for me.

If your dream feels broader than you'd like, I invite you to get curious. During the two years I spent in Washington, D.C., I soaked up every experience I could, extracting any and every bit of information I thought might be useful for my journey. I worked a series of seemingly unrelated jobs— from receptionist at a hair salon to communications manager for a homeowners' association—and in each position, I picked up new skills and knowledge that helped get me closer to realizing my vision. Along the way, I paid attention to successful female entrepreneurs whose careers inspired me. At the top of that list were two Black women who were impossible to ignore: Oprah and Beyoncé.

What grabbed my attention most about Oprah and Beyoncé wasn't even their fame or celebrated successes. It was the behind-the-scenes strategies they used to build companies that integrated both their creative goals and their world-building visions that I wanted to understand more of. I respected Beyoncé's hustle and her ability to combine a trailblazing career with creative and unexpected business moves.

My time dissecting Oprah's career was also a revelation. When I landed in D.C., Oprah was still known for her eponymous talk show, despite the fact that it had ended two years before. By that point, she had her own cable network, OWN. She developed a leadership academy for girls in South Africa. She was acting in and producing movies. She had a magazine. She even had her own food line! I was in awe of her expansiveness, her willingness to move in and out of her interests, her desires and various passions.

I spent weeks researching Oprah's history, processes, and business model and learned that every business she created fell under her umbrella company, Harpo Productions. I'd never heard of the term *umbrella company*, but as I looked into all the ventures Oprah had created under hers—including a production company that had produced the movies *Beloved*, *Precious*, and *Selma*—it dawned on me that Harpo was basically the tent under which Oprah manifested all her ideas.

It wasn't that I wanted to mimic Oprah's work, but I did want to exist as she was existing: as a Black woman with the creative freedom to see her ideas come to fruition. She was calling the shots, and she had a team of people to help execute her vision. *That's* how I wanted to exist: to be able to dream up ideas and then have a brilliant team I could work alongside to turn those ideas into a reality. However, that seemed a long way from where I was. But the seed had been planted.

One day, I would have my own umbrella company. Of course, it would take years of execution, but the power in deciding what your future can and will be is paramount to reimagining beyond the limitations often set for us.

From the outside looking in, my career plans must have seemed haphazard, and truth be told, there were days when I felt overwhelmed by the scope of what I wanted to do and the distance between here and there. But every time I had a moment to myself, I would daydream about my future success—specifically, my umbrella company. On a napkin or a scrap of paper, I'd draw the image of an umbrella and create boxes underneath. I had many ideas for what those boxes would one day contain. Sometimes I'd just lightly write out the positions I'd hope to one day fill, like CEO, lawyer, or financial officer. Sometimes I'd sketch logos for the types of service-based businesses I might be able to build and have live under my own umbrella company. These dreams took many different forms, but the basic structure always stayed the same. If I ever doubted what was possible, I would go back and study Oprah's unconventional rise to purpose and abundance.

The shape of Oprah's career showed me that it was possible for me to be more than one thing. It illustrated the ways that one's life's work can be expansive, inclusive of many passions. When I was younger, I felt silly for having so many ideas, and my friends and family would often tell me to pick one thing and do it well. My *one* thing, I decided, would be funneling my creativity and purpose into creating businesses (whatever they might be) whose mission supported women and fostered ease, access, and opportunity for marginalized groups.

I even dreamt up a name for my future company: "Loveland." The idea came to me one day while I was daydreaming about the values in which I wanted to be engulfed. And I couldn't think of a value more all-encompassing than love. A land of love. Loveland. It felt right.

When it came to planning how I'd move toward my future, I knew a nine-to-five job wouldn't serve me, as I needed flexibility not only to flesh out my entrepreneurial goals and eventually build my business, but also to care for myself, follow my curiosity, and enjoy all the things New York City had to offer. It felt risky—foolish, almost—and yet still incredibly exhilarating.

Earlier in this book, I speak about the shadow side to every reimagining. In this season, the shadows appeared as impostor syndrome, comparison to others, and doubt. When I looked at what my friends were up to—collecting degrees, finishing internships, and landing respectable positions at "important" companies and institutions—I felt like a silly young girl trying to make something out of nothing as a budding activist. Comparing my part-time jobs and babysitting to the professional careers my friends were dutifully building, I would doubt the path I was choosing for myself. *Can I really make this happen?* No one else in my world was doing what I had set out to do.

But I'd made a decision that felt true to me, based on my dreams and aspirations, so I acknowledged the presence of the shadow side, but I didn't allow that side to hijack the journey I was on. I simply stayed the course. I decided I would support myself financially with part-time jobs in fields in which I had experience, such as childcare and administrative work. That kind of work could be as flexible as I needed while pursuing my dreams of entrepreneurial success, and it was work that was almost always available.

My conviction that I didn't have to know everything to start, that I could show up green but be willing to learn, served me well. Between my jobs, I scoured social media platforms and websites such as Eventbrite for meetups and symposiums that had anything to do with entrepreneurship or building business skills and knowledge. (I had no clue what I was doing, frankly.) Then I'd sit quietly at the back of the various spaces around the city hosting these events and note the language people used, jot down the resources they mentioned, pay attention to any concepts or ideas I might need to grasp. Later, when I returned home, I'd do a deep dive on my tiny, black Google Chromebook to research it all. The podcasts, the books, the speakers, the platforms—there was so much to digest. I was hungry to understand, to be fortified by who I might become as a businesswoman.

One of the consistent messages being passed around at these meetups, symposiums, and, seemingly, on every business-focused podcast was to package and sell one's knowledge. "We're living in an information economy" is how it was explained, and we were therefore encouraged to take our expertise and turn it into an online course to create a passive income stream. But I had no interest in pretending I was a guru when I knew I wasn't, and I watched in confusion as many women did just that: *Want to earn $10K? Teach a course on how to make $10K!*

I wanted no part of a business model based on pretense. Still, I was capable of *sharing* information, and I wanted to try teaching with the new online educational platforms I'd found, to see what I could build.

Because I knew a lot about the business of babysitting from my own experience, I decided to create a course on how to be a strategic and successful babysitter. I advertised the class mostly to people I knew via my social media platform and to teens and college students back in Ohio. In total, I held my online babysitting class about five or six times, with just a handful of young women attending each session, and I loved it. I thoroughly enjoyed the opportunity to be in community with people eager to learn and take action, and with that course, I proved to myself that I could master the new technologies I was learning about through my research in entrepreneurial spaces. What's more, I felt really proud and accomplished: Instead of selling fake information, I had given my students, all young women, resources that would help them thrive. It was yet more proof that the work I was doing didn't have to be separate from the values I held or my aspirations to help women and marginalized communities. And I didn't have to create a space of exclusion as I'd seen modeled in the Girlboss realm, where women were taught to prioritize making money, as if that were a value in and of itself.

In 2016, the Girlboss and entrepreneurial world in New York City was made up overwhelmingly of white women, many of them with family wealth or wealthy husbands. I quickly realized two things. First, while I could definitely learn from the business expertise of these women, I couldn't necessarily identify with them or follow their path. Second, I needed to expand my network of mentors, teachers, and role models to include more women who looked like me and had similar backgrounds.

While attending events and reading every female-authored business book and blog was helpful, I craved an approach to entrepreneurship and empowerment that reflected my own circumstances—of not being a part of the "old boys club," not being white, not coming from wealth, not having been traditionally educated, and not possessing a business degree. I craved insight into the *kind* of business I was looking to build. I wasn't interested in the "solopreneur" lifestyle. Nor was I interested in a business career that insisted I figure out my "one thing" and then charge thousands to teach others how to do it.

As much as I would have appreciated a guidebook for the journey I was on, it was unrealistic to expect to find one, because the path I was following was one of my own making. I was operating from the belief that I, a college dropout with no cash reserves or wealthy benefactors in her family tree, could build a business that would not only sustain me, but that would exist as a revenue-generating enterprise with a social justice ethos.

That's how reimagining functions in the business arena. It's a tool that can be used to reconfigure power structures, redefine who gets a seat at the table, and challenge the status quo. Reimagining one's work means throwing out the rulebook and operating from a place of service, curiosity, passion, and desire. It means identifying one's highest values and using them—rather than mainstream society's wealth-centered values—as benchmarks for success.

PURPOSE WORK

M Y JOURNEY TO BECOMING AN ACTIVIST FOR WOMEN AND for the Black community in its entirety is the same journey that led to the beginning of my umbrella company. I just didn't know it at the time.

Remember the first time I presented my "Unpacking White Feminism" lecture at that co-working space in New York City? I charged a small fee for attendees, to help cover the cost of renting the space, and also received offers of donations toward the work I'd already done to curate the information I was sharing online. Over time, as my audience grew and lecture requests flooded in, I began receiving honorariums from the larger audiences and organizations inviting me to speak.

Slowly, as I started to earn a steady income from the work I was doing on behalf of my community, I saw more possibilities to build my business. Funny thing, though: I still didn't make the connection between my activist work and my entrepreneurial dreams. As my community continued to grow and my reputation as a public academic strengthened, it felt as though my big ideas about the "Loveland Group" were getting closer to being a reality. I just needed more hours in the day to pull it all together.

My first investment in The Loveland Group was Joe, a recent Howard University graduate turned eager manager, who'd reached out to me asking if he could offer support for what he had seen me building from afar. The truth was, I did need help. Managing a lecture schedule and keeping up with my social media content, all the while being a full-time student, left me little room to strategize, to connect all the dots and build something sustainable for myself and those learning alongside me. I would have loved to have an entire *team* to manage all I dreamed of accomplishing, but I didn't have the income to support one.

Joe and I talked, and he mentioned his own passions

toward a more ethical approach to business. We dream-shared and discussed what might be possible if I had his support. I checked in with my gut and received only good feelings, so I followed my intuition and hired him.

Technically, I hired him to be my manager, but really, he did a little bit of everything. He helped me go through emails, navigated collaboration opportunities, and often was the person organizing the details for my lectures across the country. Having Joe as my manager allowed me to lean into turning my work into a business instead of the disparate components of my passion and interests it was. Joe saw my vision and was always willing to do whatever was necessary to get me across the finish line. In fact, it was he who took the initiative to set up The Loveland Group as an actual entity by filing the necessary paperwork to create an LLC and a business bank account. That's how, in the summer of 2018, The Loveland Group was officially born.

Just to be clear, at this point in my story, The Loveland Group was just a vessel, a container for what was to come. I knew that one day it would house all the companies I dreamed up, even though I still didn't know what those companies would be. At the time, the only "company" I had existed in my lectures and online work. But just seeing the name "The Loveland Group" on the paperwork made my heart sing. My vision-casting was finally taking physical shape, and I was beginning to see the through line from my work as a lecturer, activist, and writer who centered women, women of color, and marginalized groups to anything I turned my hand to. I just had to figure out how to make it all make sense in the world, not just as a vision in my mind.

I still didn't have clarity about what my first business would be, but I did know what it would *not* be. In far too many of the entrepreneurial circles I had dipped my toe into looking for answers, there was a lot of talk of get-rich-quick schemes rather than a focus on how to creatively build a sustainable business. But I wasn't interested in selling surplus in a saturated market. I wanted to build something lasting, nourishing, transformative.

As soon as I stepped away from the oft-celebrated business models that didn't make space for who I was as a Black, queer woman who didn't come from money, I was able to reimagine something different for The Loveland Group—something that didn't have an exact blueprint but that left me feeling free and meaningful in the world.

I was deeply curious about how I might craft a business that felt bold, brilliant, and sustainable. It also had to be a business that would offer the type of lifestyle and stability I'd never had—or quite frankly ever witnessed anywhere in my family tree. I had no proof of concept that what I wanted to build could even exist, but I believed enough in my ambition, intelligence, and ability to figure things out to stay on course. And I figured that whatever the journey was going to be—even if I failed—would be better than playing small or living a life of what-ifs, like the one I'd left behind in Ohio.

THE GREAT UNLEARN

THROUGHOUT THE SPRING OF 2019, AFTER I WITHDREW from Columbia University, I focused on putting together ideas for my self-learning plan. I wanted to invite others to learn and unlearn along with me, to create an on-ramp for anyone interested in discovery, and to share my knowledge gathering in real time, empathically and in community. It made sense, given my penchant for community building and teaching as I learn. My entire adult life, I'd been bringing people along with me as I learned new skills and ideas. Whether on a virtual platform or behind a lectern, whether my subject matter was babysitting or feminism, I'd made my mark as an educator—just like young Rachel envisioned. Between my social syllabuses, my anti-racism lectures, and the teaching I imparted via my social media accounts, launching some sort of social learning platform felt like a natural progression for my work.

When the Covid-19 pandemic hit the United States in 2020, and it became clear that traveling and lecturing would be impossible, I dedicated more time to developing this self-directed learning. One night, in a burst of creativity and inspiration, it all came together in my head: I wanted to create a public education platform, one that would include an expertly curated monthly syllabus that would honor (read: appropriately compensate), center, and celebrate the work of diverse thought leaders, hosting conversations with some of the brilliant teachers I had come across in my own unlearning. I would call the platform The Great Unlearn (TGU).

With this vision fresh in my mind, I created a pitch deck containing all my ideas and shared it with my team of three: Joe and two extraordinary women, Jules and Sula, who believed in my vision and had decided to come on board with their administrative and legal expertise. Over the course of just a few months, my vision for The Great Unlearn was transformed into a reality.

It goes without saying that the Covid-19 pandemic was a tragedy of epic proportions, and it also left a lot of people alone and isolated, yearning for opportunities they could pursue from the comfort of home. While I would never say I was grateful for the pandemic, I am grateful that my company was able to provide something of value to people in their greatest time of need for community and education in the midst of the racial uprisings after the murder of George Floyd.

One of the first social syllabuses on the TGU platform focused on the truth of America's birth—the unadulterated, unromanticized origin story of our country, a nation built by slaveholders and other founders who codified chattel enslavement of Black people and who carried out a ruthless genocide against Native Americans. Given that we were in the midst of the 2020 racial uprisings, this first syllabus was particularly important, as it laid bare the fact that these weren't one-off circumstances people were protesting and demanding change around. The information we were sharing provided a historical context for the outrage we were all witnessing.

With input from a wonderful Black woman historian in the South by the name of Valerie Wade, we created a syllabus that offered both basic foundational knowledge on American history and unique perspectives, from Black people, women, and indigenous communities. The syllabus included links to public access articles and videos and questions about the material. We wanted to challenge learners to think about how to digest and apply the knowledge in ways that would activate empathy and compel action.

Within our programming we included "office hours," which included live Q&As with our experts so that our community could be in direct conversation with the people they were learning from. We also created a "study hall"—live sessions hosted by me or another facilitator where learners could come together and discuss the material, share aha moments, ask one another questions, and revisit basic academic theories and foundational texts. And we recorded everything so people could watch later, at their convenience. All this we offered as a self-paced and donation-based learning opportunity, with most learners making monthly donations of anywhere from five to five hundred dollars, based on their financial ability.

Course topics, curated to educate and inspire meaningful action, ranged from the adultification of Black girls, respectability politics, racism in healthcare, Black trans power, and nonbinary athletes. Students of TGU have reported making profound connections between the academic material, current events, and their personal circumstances, deepening their understanding of topics that aren't typically assigned or discussed, including those that reorient perspectives through a justice-focused lens.

The finished product was exactly what I'd imagined it could be, and The Great Unlearn became the first business under The Loveland Group umbrella!

AT THE SAME TIME that the world was put on hold by Covid-19, the other virus ravaging America, racism, sparked one of the largest examples of civil unrest in U.S. history. In response to the tragic yet customary Black murder-by-cop racism, Black Lives Matter protests erupted all around the country and then the world. In response, companies began waking up to the long-overdue need for diversity, equity, and inclusion training within their ranks.

Suddenly, my services as an anti-racism speaker and diversity and inclusion educator were in high demand. I was soon being booked for several large, high-impact speaking and teaching opportunities that offered substantial honorariums. While this was a powerful and exciting time in my career, it wasn't lost on me that the growth I was experiencing had come in the midst of despair. It also wasn't lost on me and many of my fellow anti-racism educators that our work was in such high demand because of the urgency felt by white America not to "seem racist." Because of this, there will always be a tint of sorrow to the origin story of The Loveland Group. I will never forget that its launch was directly tied to one of the country's deepest tragedies.

THE LOVELAND GROUP
COMES TO LIFE

WITH THE ALMOST INSTANTANEOUS SUCCESS OF THE Great Unlearn and the large jump in my speaking and teaching opportunities, I realized I had the chance to do something life-changing with the money I was making. But I didn't stash the profits away for my retirement or make any major purchases. Instead, I brought The Loveland Group fully to life by using my earnings to hire a team of full-time employees. I built out the "C-Suite" with capable people whose values and vision were aligned with my own. I then hired a CEO to lay the groundwork for the company I envisioned, to breathe life into it.

I had never felt clearer about the purpose of The Loveland Group: to live out its values in service to my community. For me personally, that meant creating an incubator for my creative business ideas; and for those I hired, it meant creating a workplace that mirrored our mission and offered tangible benefits to their lives, including comprehensive benefit packages, flexible vacation and personal time, and professional development opportunities that would serve the Loveland staff as they moved through their own personal and professional journeys. I also hired a COO to orchestrate my calendar and partnerships, and help build the matrix of relationships that made up our extended community, including our collaborators, sponsors, and the organizations we'd often support.

That choice, to invest in a team who then built out the entire foundation of The Loveland Group based on my vision and my values, was the best decision I could have ever made. This build-out happened as seamlessly as it did because, over the many years of dreaming up The Loveland Group, I'd attracted all the right components to bring my vision to fruition once my time came. It was like flipping a switch and watching the lights come on.

Once I had a full and committed team involved, we were able to continue to build out the work done within The Great Unlearn. With the team's sustainable management of

my speaking and teaching calendar leaving me room to envision what came next, it wasn't long before my dreaming
heart activated again, and by the fall of 2020, The Loveland
Group was bringing to life another dream of mine: to open
a bookstore.

I called it Elizabeth's Bookshop and Writing Centre.
("Elizabeth" is my middle name, the name that, when I was
a child, I always wanted to be called. The name, therefore, is
a gift to my younger self.) Because of the Covid-19 lockdowns, we started as an online bookstore, but once it was
safe to do so, we opened a physical location in Akron. The
bookshelves at Elizabeth's are filled with the works of authors usually marginalized in or excluded from the cultural
canon (Black, queer, indigenous, etc.). The Writing Centre
offers workshops and programming to celebrate the creativity and literary craftmanship of these communities.

My entrepreneurial spirit was satisfied to see Elizabeth's
and TGU flourish. I didn't see these entities as businesses in
the traditional sense, but as a reimagining of what for-profit
ventures could be and do.

THE LOVELAND FOUNDATION

During this time, I also cemented the launch of
The Loveland Foundation, the nonprofit charitable arm
of The Loveland Group whose mission is to provide free
mental health therapy for Black women and girls. So many
Black women, girls, and gender-expansive folks find themselves in need of therapy but without the financial resources

to access quality care. This was the painful situation I myself had faced in my early years in New York City, when I was without health insurance and forced to simply "wait out" my depression.

The price of not having supportive health resources when they are needed is too high for anyone to have to pay. The Office of Minority Health (part of the U.S. Department of Health and Human Services) reported that Black teenagers were more likely to attempt suicide than white teenagers, and Black people living below the poverty line were three times more likely to report serious psychological distress than those living above the poverty line.

With The Loveland Foundation, what started as a one-off fundraising campaign to support Black women's mental health had morphed into an ambitious organization that paired Black women and girls with Black therapists at no cost to the patient and with no proof of need required. While I understand that not everyone finds benefits in the type of talk therapy the foundation provides access to, I felt deeply that those who wanted and needed it should have an easy and affordable path to receiving it. In the United States and even the rest of the Western world today, this is not the case for the majority of Black women and girls and gender-expansive people, and the gap in mental health care between Black and white America is stark.

The Loveland Foundation was created—reimagined, actually—at the intersection of deep community need and my highest values, and we exist in a way that centers Black women, girls, and gender-expansive people in the ecosystem of emotional and psychological wellness. Our founding staff is comprised entirely of Black women, and as of this writing, we have offered over one hundred thousand hours of therapy to more than twelve thousand participants. I am both inspired and deeply grateful that we were able to turn this vision into a reality.

A VALUES-BASED BUSINESS

THE LOVELAND GROUP GREW IN PHASES, IN FITS AND starts, taking both baby steps and giant leaps. Today, it's a full ecosystem of ventures staffed by brilliant, empathetic, powerful people who identify as women, queer, of color, and as various other unique identities that add to the genius they bring to the table.

Both The Loveland Group and The Loveland Foundation are fueled by my highest values of ease, abundance, and opportunity, which feed into one another. Under the Loveland Group umbrella sits The Great Unlearn, The Great Unlearn for Young Learners, Elizabeth's Bookshop and Writing Centre, and what I call the Office of Rachel Cargle, which handles the business side of my speaking and consulting work (such as my "Unpacking White Feminism" lectures and my DEI [diversity, equity, and inclusion] consulting) and my writing. The Loveland Foundation operates independently, with its own donors and revenue sources, but it also collaborates intentionally with The Loveland Group ventures in various ways to build community and raise both awareness and funding for our services.

Every iteration of the Loveland ecosystem is nourished

by the fruits of each individual branch. The Loveland Foundation also receives a minimum of 10 percent of everything that crosses the profit line from the business side, whether that's from a book purchase through Elizabeth's, my own speaking and consulting work, or subscriptions for TGU.

I share the story of The Loveland Group here, and the details of how it is made up and run, as a real-world example of how big dreams can be built on passion and sustained by curiosity and values. I know this might sound impractical and unrealistic when compared to what a hyper-capitalist, patriarchal world understands business to be. But what I've learned through the ups and downs of my own professional journey, and what I know from my soul and from experience, is that values *can* be the driving force of your life's work. I truly believe that a focus on your highest values, even while you juggle multiple gigs to get by, will offer you the best chance to achieve your professional dreams—whether that's an office in the C-Suite, a promotion at your current job, or the freedom to work under the shade of a swaying palm tree. Focusing on what makes sense to your soul will give you a life in which you are fully seated, one you can be proud to have built yourself.

It's not always easy, but my hope is that by taking the time to home in on your highest values and consider them in relation to your work, you can arrive at a place where your work has more intentionality, both as you perform it and in how you position it in your life. Yes, we live in a capitalistic society—there's currently no way around that—but we have the power to reimagine how we show up in this society and how we contribute through our work.

———

A JUSTICE-ORIENTED CALLING AND my highest values of ease, abundance, and opportunity are woven into the fabric of The Loveland Group and all its branches, and we ensure that those values show up in our partnerships, our goal-setting, and in how the staff exist with one another. My goal as the visionary is for our values to be applied rigorously and seriously to create practices and systems that enable the company, the employees, and anyone with whom we interact to walk the walk. Our values are tools and lenses that help us decide how to use resources—not only money, which is just one type of resource, but also time, energy, expertise, and relationships. These values guide us and those we partner with to operate in ways that are communal and founded on trust and a shared vision of equity.

What if you applied your values rigorously to your own work? If one of your values happens to be ease, maybe this means you bring a level of intention and strategy to your work flow systems, allowing for more efficiency in your workday. If community is a highest value for you, perhaps you join (or start!) a monthly lunch group of aligned professionals within or outside your workplace for encouragement and idea sharing. While my journey has been entrepreneurship, a values-based approach is applicable to various forms of work. Sure, you might not be able to change a company's values, but you can bring your own values to the table as you work.

The protocols in place that guide The Loveland Group's operating procedures—from the practices that support the staff's work-life balance, to work flow systems, to our relationships with collaborators—are, essentially, matriarchal. While a patriarchal system uses domination and concentrates power in individuals at the top, in a matriarchal system, the power comes from within. It is the values set by the organization and the people in it, rather than outside forces, that dictate practices. The matriarchy at Loveland has less to do with gender and more with the way the business is framed—as a matriarchal system rooted in practices that focus on sustainability and the health of the group as a whole. Every person has unique gifts and experiences, and instead of requiring that employees conform to inflexible ways of working or existing that are preset by society, we invite individuals at our company to help shape Loveland's practices with their one-of-a-kind expertise.

Matriarchal systems—which have existed for hundreds of thousands of years in many societies and are still in existence, primarily in indigenous cultures—center the actual humans carrying out the work, as opposed to centering the labor they are doing. (At Loveland, we consider our employees the "human force" instead of the "labor force.") The labor is of value, too, of course, but it does not exist independently of the people who do it.

The Loveland Group is constantly evolving, growing, and adapting because that's what humans do; we are not static or one-dimensional. Our lives and relationships and moods and bodies shift, and I believe it's important that all businesses allow for and embrace these fluctuations. Within a matriarchal business structure, we strive for receptivity among staff, regardless of job title or role, for an environment that feels nurturing, supportive, and open—in contrast to the patriarchy's top-down system, where only bosses are decision makers. That's not to say there isn't a boss lady—that would be me—but my role is primarily to guide with my vision. I mentor, I trust, and very often I learn from my staff.

In addition, Loveland operates with a moral compass that calibrates us away from the capitalist, do-more, make-more, acquire-more mantras. Our metrics for success are not dollars and cents or output, but whether we are achieving our goals (whatever those may be at a given stage) in ways that offer ease, abundance, and opportunity for our staff, those we serve (namely, Black women and the LGBTQ+ community), and those we collaborate with. Although my company exists within the capitalist economic structure of the United States, we seek as much as possible to flourish outside this intrinsically racist, misogynist system.

A hallmark of capitalism is its instability, and when the market crashes—which it does, like clockwork, every four to seven years—it is women, people of color, and the poor who take the hit. I am writing these sentences during the Covid-19 pandemic, in the midst of an inflation crisis, and one of the undeniable lessons from both is that the most vulnerable in our society are always the first economic casualties. Of those who lost their jobs or saw their income reduced during 2020 and 2021, the majority were Black, Hispanic, and of lower income. And in December 2020, according to the Bureau of Labor Statistics, all the job losses were of those held by women—all 140,000 of them. And most of those jobs had been held by women of color.

Loveland is creating and reimagining a world in which these inequalities and cruelties would never have a chance to exist. Along with many other justice-oriented individuals, grassroots organizations, and companies committed to ethical entrepreneurship, we are forging a new way to do business. Our company policies are all intended to be a reimagining of how one can exist in a workplace, one that offers space for all human experiences (from giving birth, to caring for those close to death, to experiencing joy, illness, wellness, rest, and beyond) to align harmoniously. Our highest values are the tools of our craft, and we wield them with power and love.

My hope is that regardless of where you fall in our economic ecosystem, whether you are a power broker or making your way in the gig economy, you recognize the opportunities to make a difference. Those who sit at the head of companies and organizations can reimagine and implement more ethical ways of business management, fairer treatment of their employees and the communities they serve. You don't have to wait for someone else to do it first.

However, if you find yourself with little access to the keys to the corporate kingdom, you can also use your reimagination muscle to find ways to advocate for yourself, your fellow workers, and your community. Remember, the cost of reimagining is free, but the results can be invaluable, and life-changing.

To be clear, we at The Loveland Group do not shun the idea of money and profit—it's the price of admission to live and work in a capitalist economic system—but we don't view money as the most important resource. Expertise, relationships, intention, time, energy—there is a wellspring of resources from which to draw to push any project forward. For us, there is no one way to accomplish a goal; nor is there a single way to define "success." In fact, the concepts of success and failure are too all-or-nothing to exist in a space of abundance. Outside the restrictive binary of success and failure is a mindset of growth, of learning, of exploration and possibility.

There are a thousand and one ways to be well as a company and as individuals, and in the ecosystem of Loveland, we allow for many routes. Of course, there must be specific, well-defined goals and systems. And when something isn't working, we face the music and shift gears, recalibrating. But that recalibrating is done with trust that there will always be a way forward and support from the myriad relationships braided into and nourished within the Loveland community.

A DREAM REALIZED

WHEN I LOOK AT THE LOVELAND GROUP FROM THE ten-thousand-foot perspective, I see my napkin sketch come to life. It exists exactly as I envisioned it—as an umbrella company that houses many beautiful and flourishing ventures with diverse iterations, reaches, and audiences, all of them grounded in the values the staff and I cradle, values that help us reimagine the world in ways that nourish my community.

When I look back on my journey to this place as an entrepreneur, as a businesswoman sitting at the helm of a company she conjured up from her wildest imaginings, I remember where I came from—and I am in awe. I have the opportunity to do work in the world that means so much to me. I have the resources to take care of my mother as she ages. I am funneling tens of thousands of dollars into ventures that provide opportunities for Black women and girls and others who are often marginalized, kept from opportunity, resources, and celebration. I am running my businesses according to my highest values of ease, abundance, and opportunity, and doing so demands that those with whom Loveland collaborates hold those values as well, ensuring that we're all promoting justice, equality, liberation, and joy. And we are doing it all with a different set of goalposts than those in the usual capitalist model, which seeks to expand for the sake of expansion and which prioritizes labor and profit above community and equality.

I have not only reimagined my own entrepreneurial existence, but I have built it, as much as possible, outside the traditional, limiting, racist structures that have been handed to us by a patriarchal, white supremacist culture. My journey has been both incredibly complicated and unexpectedly wonderful, and I am proud of myself for getting this far.

But I don't believe there is only one way to go about achieving your dreams. Everyone has their own path to take. My hope is that by explaining how *I* did it, you might see what is possible. My hope is that you will draw inspiration, finding little or big lessons in my experiences, and that as you pursue your dream, you will feel my gaze and hear my voice saying, *Keep going*.

ROAD MAP TO YOUR RENAISSANCE: REIMAGINING WORK

THROUGHOUT THIS CHAPTER, I'VE SHARED MY STORY OF building my business, starting with nothing more than a vision and the belief in my own ability to continuously reimagine what was possible. My ideas about what The Loveland Group could be, and the resulting business I created, came not from imitating existing structures or pathways to success, but from braiding in my highest values and bypassing traditional education, funding sources, and limiting beliefs about what a Black woman could accomplish.

You, too, can use your reimagination to vision-cast a version of work that nourishes you, enriches your life, and sets your soul on fire. You are not beholden to the "way it has always been done." I'm giving you permission now to reimagine the work you do in the world so that it serves *you* first.

Of course, there are many ways for us to "do our work" in the world. Entrepreneurship was my way, but it is not the only way; nor should it be viewed as the best way, even when you are trying to bring new ideas to fruition. Many other successful people work *within* existing organizations or institutions, and even in those spaces there is a chance to honor and hone our values. There *is* opportunity to reimagine new structures, new protocols, new systems that prioritize quality over quantity, service over sales, and people over profit. It *is* possible to do work that comes to you with ease and that fills you with joy rather than dread. Imagine what that would feel like! Imagine feeling purposeful every day when you go to work, defining work in a way that is meaningful to you.

That being said, it is critical that I stress that the thing you find as "your work" in the world doesn't have to be the thing you do to make a living. It is a nasty trick of capitalism to make us believe that the only places we are allowed to feel purposeful are in the spaces where our efforts earn us money. I know many people who clock out of their jobs to head to their home studios, their churches, their volunteer groups, and various other spaces where they focus on what feels like their life's work. For a passion to be of value, it is not a requirement that it make you money. When I say "reimagine work," I am not insisting that you simply "reimagine how to make a profit." I want to encourage you to reimagine adding to your world, your community, and your life experience in a way that is expansive, aligned, and true to you.

Consider how the following will help you reimagine work for yourself:

FIND A HOME FOR YOUR HIGHEST VALUES. Consider where you might infuse your highest values into your current work space. If you value rest, for example, this might look like setting clear boundaries around how late you will stay at the office. Or, it could be a policy you introduce for others—for example, allowing women to work from home when they have their period. Revisit your highest values and see how they can be incorporated into your work life.

REVISIT YOUR CHILDHOOD DREAMS. If you're still trying to decide what you want to be when you grow up,
whether you are twenty-two or fifty-two, ask yourself,
*What are things I remember really wanting to achieve or
pursue when I was a child, a teenager, and a twenty-year-
old?* What still resonates from those memories now,
and how can you find large or small ways to try on
those goals? If you wanted to be a teacher, can you
volunteer at a community center on weekends or
teach a class at the local community college? If you
always dreamed of being a dancer, or a painter, find a
class and tap back into that joy to see where it leads
you. The key is to get yourself back into your dreams
and see what comes to pass.

EMULATE YOUR HEROES. Consider the careers of people you admire. What "clues" can you gather to help
curate a career that feels good to you? What meat can
you find from what others have cooked up and created? What bones will you throw away to make that
career uniquely yours? I studied Oprah's career like a
treasured recipe, but I added my own ingredients and
came up with my own unique "dish." Remember, it's
never too late to start building your dream career or
job. No matter what stage we're at in life, we all owe
ourselves the opportunity to reinvent, shape-shift, and
pursue possibilities.

REIMAGINE "SUCCESS." Really consider what success
at work means beyond a substantial paycheck or a

solid benefits package. Think about the domino effect that can come from your financial stability and "success" within your communities. If you are successful, what can you do to turn around on the ladder and help the woman on the rung beneath you? How can you connect your work to the needs of others? Sometimes it's not the work itself that requires reimagining, but how you can use the output from your labor to do something meaningful in the world, something that sparks a movement, makes an impact, or simply blankets somebody in comfort and care.

MAPPING YOUR
OWN MANIFESTO

· ·

I have found my work in the world to be rooted in using **my genius as an activist, writer, entrepreneur, and philanthropic innovator.** I do my work in a way that aligns with my values and desires.

What is *your* work rooted in? What do you want the work you do in the world to look like and be about? What comes easily to you? Substitute the text in boldface with your own description of work that is unique and meaningful to you.

CHAPTER 6

REIMAGINING REST

...

IRONICALLY, WHILE I WAS DEVOTING SO MUCH OF MY energy to building The Loveland Foundation throughout 2019, inspired to create a place for Black women to heal, I faltered on caring for my own mental health. My launching of the foundation was eclipsed only by the whirlwind of 2020.

Between the racial uprisings and the Covid-19 pandemic, my brain was firing on all cylinders. I was trying to balance my speaking engagements, my online community, and the work of building my company and the foundation. Despite the world's "officially slowing down" as lockdowns took place across the country, my own world sped up . . . and has only grown more intense since then. As an anti-racism educator in high demand, I felt compelled to show up despite my fears, mounting anxiety, and stress. Eventually, I had to stop. I *needed* to stop. I needed to rest.

RECLAIMING REST

I ONCE READ THAT ALBERT EINSTEIN DREAMT UP THE theory of relativity *not* in front of an equation-covered chalkboard, but during a moment of relaxation . . . while riding a bicycle.

It makes perfect sense. For me, moments when my brain can take a pause from intensive thinking and meander on its own a bit, are often when the magic happens. Unencumbered by "serious" thought, I find little jewels of illumination—epiphanies my friend EbonyJanice likes to call "casual brilliance"—floating up and finding their way into my consciousness.

A few years ago, EbonyJanice and I were having brunch at a restaurant in Harlem when she shared with me a question she'd sat with and discussed many times but that was new to me: "What would we be doing with our lives, with our brains, our brilliance, if we were not so busy trying to survive whiteness?" she probed. "What would you be writing about, Rachel?"

I thought about it. "Maybe romance novels, or a YA series about little Black girls who can talk to animals. Or gardening. I'm not sure." Then I turned the question back to her: "What would *you* be doing if you never had to do this work?"

"I wouldn't be working at all. I'd be resting and rendez-vousing with a lover."

For the remainder of our brunch date, we dreamt together of all the alternative ways we could exist in the world if our lives weren't so consumed by our struggle against the assaults of racism, sexism, and productivity-obsessed capital-ism.

Over the next few weeks, I couldn't shake our conversa-tion. I was devoting most of my time, energy, and career to fighting white supremacy, a lifesaving calling I'd never *not* do, but it had been a while since I opened up to the many other ways I could be using my mental resources, my time, my talents; or ways that I could simply be resting and find-ing pleasure.

I imagine that most Black people reading this are nod-ding their heads. Surviving white supremacy can be all-consuming. From the classroom to the boardroom to the loan office to the medical clinic, it co-opts your mental re-sources. The late, great writer Toni Morrison warned of the insidious, all-consuming nature of living with racism:

> The function, the very serious function, of racism is distraction . . . It keeps you from doing your work. It keeps you explaining over and over again your reason for being. Somebody says you have no language so you spend twenty years proving that you do . . . Somebody says you have no art, so you dredge that up. Somebody says you have no kingdoms, so you dredge that up. None of that is necessary. There will always be one more thing.

Racism doesn't need to be blatant to take a toll. A micro-aggression—a subtly racist comment from a co-worker ("Wow, you're so articulate!?") or having someone reach out to touch your hair—can hijack your mental energy. You spend hours thinking about whether to let it go or to confront it, running through the "choose your own racial justice adventure" options in your head. Then you spend another span of time parsing the decision: Did what you said teach her anything? Or did it just bring *you* more stress? Then you get on the phone with your friend or partner to vent about it for a while. Before you know it, large chunks of your day are gone—not to mention the spike in stress hormones.

After that conversation with EbonyJanice, I also contemplated the idea of productivity and achievement and how we correlate self-worth with acts of grandiosity: winning a medal, changing the world, making everyone proud, leaving a lasting legacy. Why can't life be lived simply—finding joy, learning from pain, and holding ourselves accountable? Being good to others. Relishing the wonder of it all and riding this thing out.

The ideas of Black excellence and Black girl magic, while affirming in some instances, can also be something of a frustration to the Black community. It asks that we be extraordinary, often in relation to whiteness, when we deserve to live our lives and retain our dignity whether we are winning Olympic gold medals or simply raising our families in Middle America.

Before that conversation with EbonyJanice, my perception of rest and productivity was like most people's: a combination of my family upbringing and the culture that fed me ideas about the intersection of self-worth and output. It is capitalism that ushered in the belief that we are here on earth only to produce goods or services, to extract value from our time, and to derive our self-worth from what we *do* as opposed to who we *are*. Because of this, many of us grapple with guilt around our need for rest, as though rest or stillness were a waste of time.

I grew up very aware that my family was on government assistance. I have terrible memories of my mother cleaning frantically at all hours in case an agent of the state, authorized to visit and observe Section 8 housing whenever they wanted, dropped in to assess how many people were living in our home. The government also required that we share our financial records with it, and if our bank balances were over a certain amount, the excess would be reflected in a rent increase. So, our government "help" came in the form of surveillance and control, a policing of the poor in a system that gives those who are struggling no space to truly thrive. And despite the public assistance we received, there were many times when we had to stand in line at various churches for free groceries when we didn't have enough to eat.

Recently, I was able to move my mother into an apartment and put her rent on autopay. Finally, after decades of living from hand to mouth and worrying about where every dollar went, she can relax and rest. But she almost doesn't know how. She can hardly believe we have even the slightest bit of security. It's almost as if she has imposter syndrome, as if she feels she doesn't deserve to live peacefully and confidently.

The stereotype of the strong, Black woman, she who can persevere and overcome anything and everything, while inspiring and true to some extent, can also work against us, embedding in our psyches the false notion that we aren't allowed to ask for help or to take a break when our physical or mental health is in jeopardy. With the added burden of surviving whiteness, what many Black women are *not* doing enough of—what *I* was not doing enough of—is resting, daydreaming, communing with other Black women, caring for themselves in ways that replenish them and open up paths to different, joyful ways of existing, thinking, and dreaming.

Black people often spend so much time imagining death, fearing death, preparing themselves for the possibility of premature death for themselves or their family members—death by police violence, homicide, disease—that it can be an ever-present mental passenger. But we have good reason to fear death. We have a lower life expectancy than our white counterparts. In 2020, Black Americans' life expectancy was seventy-two years compared to seventy-eight years for white Americans, a gap that widened during the Covid-19 pandemic. Black mothers are especially vulnerable. In New York City, where I live, Black women have the highest rate of maternal death (387 per 10,000 deliveries), which is three times that for white women (127 per 10,000 deliveries). And even when one accounts for similar risk factors, such as low educational attainment, neighborhood poverty, and pre-pregnancy obesity, this disparity persists.

There's a line in Lin-Manuel Miranda's musical *Hamilton* that describes, for me, the disproportionate space the concept of death takes up in a Black person's psyche: "I imagine death so much, it feels more like a memory." I was so tired of imagining death and surviving whiteness. I was ready to be engaged with living in a way that invited exuberance and optimism, to sit in comfortable stillness and to relax and dream—not as a way to escape an awful or dangerous reality, but to reimagine glorious possibilities from a place of creativity, clarity, and freedom. The truth is, the act of fantasizing, of allowing yourself to notice and indulge what nourishes you and drives your happiness and satisfaction, is not an idle pursuit. It is the very opposite: It has the potential to be the bedrock of your next reimagined existence.

This question is for most readers, but particularly for Black women: When do you feel entitled to rest, to daydream, to indulge? After you've accomplished a full day's work? After you've accomplished a full *week's* work? A *year's*? Or—according to the average retirement age—nearly a lifetime? Do you think of downtime and self-care as rewards or as something you can do only when you're on the cusp of a breakdown?

I've always hustled, and I've relished it—for the most part. The glory of possibility has almost always sustained me. And I certainly wouldn't have achieved what I have without putting in many hours, days, months, and years of hard work. When I first arrived in New York City, I juggled four jobs. I worked the front desk of a children's play space, had a part-time position doing administrative work for a major marketing firm in Manhattan, balanced a slew of babysitting gigs, and used most of my early mornings and late nights developing a business plan for my entrepreneurial pursuits.

Though I was feeling grateful for the experience of chasing my dreams, I was not able to show up as my best self in any of these individual areas because my body and mind could take only so much pressure and still remain present and perform well. As I dug deeper into learning about the intersection of race and womanhood, I came to view rest and self-care not as optional or reward-oriented, but as necessities for myself.

I have come to see rest as a human right.

GIVING MY ACTIVISM A REST

As I CONTINUED TO PUT REST IN ITS PROPER PLACE IN my life, I couldn't help but turn a lens of discovery toward my commitment to activism and social justice work. By the end of 2021, it felt as though I'd turned myself inside out in an effort to keep up with the ever-increasing demand for activists to lead the fight against racism, white supremacy, and the ever-present patriarchy. I had entered this arena as a community builder and then became an educator, but increasingly in my daily work, I felt like a soldier going to war.

My life had become a series of anxieties and worries about things I had no control over: Thousands of people were arguing on my social media accounts, expecting me to provide critical commentary or the answer to an unsolvable problem. I'd show up in Trump-country towns to deliver a lecture even after receiving death threats from locals who'd heard I was coming. People demanded that I speak about, metabolize, and react to the never-ending parade of racial violence flashing through the news cycle. All of it depleted every ounce of energy I had.

The thing is, while it seemed that I'd somewhat mastered the *idea* of rest in my daily routines, I hadn't been as successful at incorporating this form of self-care into my activism work. The rapid pace, and accompanying intensity, of the country's descent into its racial reckoning had me and every other person working in the field of racial justice in emergency mode, leaving little time for rest or reflection.

But the fight was killing me. I was so exhausted that my physical health began to deteriorate. My immune system was in tatters, and I was getting sick with a frequency I had never experienced. I had aches and pains in my back and neck that no chiropractor seemed to be able to address. My nervous system was also a mess, what with the anxiety and pressure of my being in the public eye. I tell people now that I had "racial PTSD." I was getting triggered by white people, particularly if they entered what I considered my safe spaces. I would literally have a physical reaction of fear and then aggression toward their whiteness.

That's when I knew I had to step away from how I was approaching the work.

"YOU ARE THE ONE YOU'RE FIGHTING FOR"

Ebonyjanice once said to me, "you are the black woman you are fighting for." Her words now haunted me, and I was forced to think about how I was showing up for the movement.

I imagined a Black woman saying to me, "I'm tired. I need to rest. I can't do this anymore." My response to her would never be: "Your exhaustion doesn't matter. Just stay out there and keep doing the work. Work until you can't work anymore." But if I would never treat someone else that way, why was I putting that kind of pressure on myself as an activist? The answer is: I shouldn't have. The answer is: I won't put those expectations on myself anymore. Instead, I had to reimagine how I could show up as an activist.

Like the model of the starving artist, there is a Western concept of the perpetually angry activist, a person who must live a life that is both humble and impoverished. There is no defined space where being well, feeling abundant, and doing public service can typically coexist. But why must the activist suffer in order to be considered legitimate? I refuse to believe that, in my effort to serve my community, struggle is a prerequisite for rest. I reject any idea that suggests we must earn the right simply to *be* in the world.

I noticed, in my own career, that people wanted to see me in a state of agitation, having heated conversations with white women, showing up as the angry Black woman activist. What's more, they were skeptical of my authenticity when I chose to care for myself. If I wasn't causing a fuss over one thing or another, or if I dared show up in public extolling the virtues of rest and self-care (which I did on occasion), I was deemed less than authentic in the role of activist.

In recognizing my positionality in anti-racism spaces, in feminist spaces, I realized that it wasn't sustainable, and it wasn't where I wanted to be anymore. I wanted to take a moment to pivot away from the fight against white supremacy and the patriarchy and calibrate my work toward the intentional nourishment and celebration of Black women instead.

I wanted to reimagine the role I could play as activist, feminist, and supporter and champion of Black women. I wanted to reimagine a way I could show up for my community without running myself ragged. I wanted to reimagine the role of the activist. She is well-rested, joyful, but still effective in doing the work. I wanted to reimagine it, so I did.

Today, I am happily in a new space of work that no longer involves trying to change the minds and behavior of white people. The truth is, I have lost hope in whiteness ever changing. I made a decision to focus instead on rest and ease for Black women and other marginalized people. I'm going to grasp at and revel in and be indulgent with any type of goodness I can access while I'm here on this earth. And I am going to do my best to get other people—my people—access to all that goodness, too. Because, as Langston Hughes said, "I do not need my freedom when I'm dead."

I don't regret any part of the work I've done over the last five years. I'm proud of it. I think that my approach to addressing issues of racism within the feminist movement played its small role in the movement toward racial justice and women's empowerment. I feel very proud of the contributions I made in that lane. That work was necessary and meaningful, but now my work reflects more of my desires for both powerful contribution and soft and sustainable living.

CHAMPIONING REST

I HAVE THE CONNECTIONS I'VE MADE ON SOCIAL MEDIA to thank for my reorientation around rest, work, and productivity. One day a few years ago, most likely in the midst of one of those wildly busy days, I came across the account of the Nap Ministry, founded by Tricia Hersey, a Black performance artist, theologian, and community activist. After EbonyJanice's "casually brilliant" question about what we'd be doing if we weren't trying to survive whiteness prompted me to reexamine my ideas around work and rest, I read some of the Nap Ministry's posts:

> "Rest is resistance because it pushes back against capitalism and white supremacy."

> "Black women! You are not the mules of the world, you can rest."

> "You don't have to earn rest."

> "Sleep deprivation is a social justice issue."

Something clicked into place. This mindset, this *knowledge,* felt transformative. It strengthened my resolve to turn away from an existence of nonstop productivity punctuated by infrequent periods of rest and to turn toward a more intentional pace—one that gave space not only for downtime but for me to acknowledge my dignity outside what I produced in the world. This led to my adopting a different attitude toward rest and self-care in both my personal life *and* my social justice pursuits—which, EbonyJanice has always pointed out to me, are often one and the same. "Rachel, you do so much work fighting for the ease and rest of Black women," she would say. "You can't forget that you, too, are a Black woman."

Recognizing that resting and self-care were braided into my life's most important work—reclaiming for Black women and girls what we deserve—allowed me to say no to many things without guilt: No to collaboration requests with a quick turnaround. No to social invitations on the nights I just wanted to fall into bed and sleep. It also meant leaning into saying yes to the things that thrilled me. Yes to doing something daring, like walking in New York Fashion Week. Yes to the invitation to write fun, light pieces for magazines, like the piece I crafted exploring the legacy of Black cowboys in American history.

By looking at my work and life habits through this new lens, I became aware of the busy-ness I'd engaged in without intention—like responding instantly to texts or checking my email from bed first thing every morning. I started questioning whether these tasks truly served me and my goals or were simply keeping me in a never-ending whirlpool of work.

How to Do Nothing: Resisting the Attention Economy, by Jenny Odell, is a brilliant companion for anyone looking to slow down, defy the attention economy, and curb an addiction to pointless productivity. "Our very idea of productivity is premised on the idea of producing something new, whereas we do not tend to see maintenance and care as productive in the same way," Odell explains. It was time for me to zero in on that maintenance and care.

I paid close attention to what gave me joy during my days. I took note of the things that nourished me, so that I could incorporate these more indulgent behaviors into my days with the same regularity as the other habits I engaged in for my maintenance. Getting in a thirty-minute nap each day or taking time each morning to stretch my body soon fell into cadence with things like grocery shopping or brushing my teeth. I would no longer allow my tank to get to Empty before I filled it; nor would I wait until I was bone-tired before "rewarding" myself with downtime. Better yet, at times, I would give myself the option to do nothing.

I now regarded proactively reclaiming rest and self-care as my birthright, believing that it would allow for a different type of existence; would usher in feelings, thoughts, and re-imaginings that, in the go-go-go of modern life, hadn't yet had the opportunity to be birthed and to flourish. In the same way that a parent observes what makes her child happy, I studied Rachel with deep empathy, loving scrutiny, and a spirituality rooted in understanding myself. We must all engage in this kind of personal study as we evolve.

I began studying my moods and emotional cycles: What restored me? What drained me? Who was pouring energy into me, and who was not? I had to sit with my feelings to understand them—instead of rushing through them, which often feels easier but is less helpful to our growth.

For me, therapy also played a major role in this self-study. Each element of our lives plays a part in what we believe we deserve, and with the help of a professional therapist, I could address my flaws, my emotional walls, and my childhood trauma.

Here's what I learned:

I find so much joy in the simplicity of what I call "the

living." At times, the rhythm of folding my laundry or the slow pace of chopping vegetables for a homemade meal feels as rewarding as making strides in my work. This, too, is where the goodness of existing lives.

I implemented an easeful morning routine, a way of waking up to the day with tasks and rituals that make me happy: tidying up my space (I'm a morning cleaner) and watering my plants, listening to jazz, burning a favorite candle all before I eased into my first work meetings of the day. New hobbies, like throwing pottery and learning French, have given my days more light and texture. This joy, this ease, this rest—all this, too, is part of the meaningful work I might do in this lifetime.

Other approaches to relaxing include tapping, a self-soothing technique based on Chinese acupressure points, which can calm a person in minutes, if not seconds. Taking time throughout the day simply to breathe or meditate can make a profound difference in one's mood, bringing feelings of well-being. Deep breathing instantly activates the vagus nerve, which runs from the brain stem through the lungs and heart and into the diaphragm. When we inhale and exhale deeply and fully, we send a signal via the vagus nerve to our brain to calm our fight-or-flight response and pump the brakes on stress hormones.

Of course, rest and relaxation don't have to be planned, and they don't have to include therapy or some sort of activity. We can give ourselves permission simply to be, to exist, to build into our days moments of doing nothing—whether that means lighting incense and closing your eyes for thirty minutes or gazing out your living room window and day-dreaming for long spans of time. I began giving myself scheduled blocs for rest that didn't always look like sleep. Sometimes I'll just lie on my couch, close my eyes, and listen to jazz, letting my mind enjoy the artistry. Taking a walk to the botanical garden near my apartment, and intentionally leaving my phone at home, is also as productive as networking within my industry and among my peers.

Once I gave myself the gift of just being, I suddenly prioritized things I'd been putting off—such as curating the children's book collection of my personal library, so I'd always have a really good story to read when visiting friends brought their little ones with them. I did this not because it checked some preordained task off a list, but because being a part of a village that raises these beautiful humans is as sweet and valuable as the effort I put into building my career.

During this reimagining of rest, it also became clear to me that spending time with other Black women, a communing that fed me in a way nothing else could, had to be elevated to the top of my to-do list. Being with my sister-friends is where I feel safest, most understood. Sharing our stories is a form of therapy. Seeing and hearing from one another is a permission slip for all of us to feel less alone, less vulnerable, more fortified, freer.

I had been spending so much time engaging with white people in my lecture spaces and online that I needed intentional nourishment from and with my community. So, I opened up my calendar and filled in several months' worth of weekend morning coffee dates (by phone or in person), both with friends I'd dropped the ball on and new friends I was looking forward to getting to know better. I positioned myself to find any and every way I could to build on these meaningful connections. I stocked a picnic basket with plates, utensils, and cups and stashed it in the trunk of my car, so that if I ran into a friend on the street or at a store, we could grab a quick bite together in a nearby park—taking advantage of another thing that gives me pleasure: the beauty of nature. When I went apartment-hunting in Brooklyn, I chose a home with an outdoor space where I could do things like gather friends for an evening dinner, or host a tiny terrace audience for a friend's poetry reading. A space for community right there in my home.

COMMUNITY REST

As I began to intentionally incorporate these rituals into my life, I became better at setting boundaries around times of rest. There was simply no glory in being busy all the time, and my value as a person was not tied to how much I could accomplish in a day.

One weekend, while on a romantic rendezvous at a Getaway cabin—Getaway is a company that provides simple, beautifully appointed wooden cabins in natural settings around the country for quick escapes from city life—I had a moment of pause. As I was experiencing solace and relaxation in the quiet of the woods, the kind of healing that only Mother Nature can provide, I realized that this type of

nature-based, restorative experience would be a healing balm
for Black activists, organizers, and educators who were ex-
pending so much of themselves for our collective liberation.
They deserved a place like this, somewhere they could turn
off, tune out, and reconnect with themselves or with loved
ones. They deserved a place where, if they so desired, they
could do absolutely nothing.

I reached out to the Getaway team to share my ideas and
insights into how their company could show up for the Black
community. Just a few short months after connecting, brain-
storming, and getting our ideas onto paper, I was thrilled to
announce The Loveland Group's partnership with Getaway.
The program we dreamt up together, called 100 Nights of
Rest, would award to Black folks working for change a free
night's stay at a Getaway accommodation, reimbursed travel
costs, and a food stipend. From doulas to artists to environ-
mentalists to LBGTQ+ community organizers to therapists
to healthcare workers fighting Covid-19—the recipients of
these Getaway getaways (nominated by friends, colleagues,
and family) were able to reclaim a little bit of rest that, we
hoped, would follow them back to their day-to-day existences. The response to the program was so phenomenal that
we expanded, renaming it "A Year of Rest," to try to serve as
many people as possible.

I even took the concept of rest into The Loveland Group.
In the hope that the company I founded might have longev-
ity far past my time running it, I knew rest had to be centered and celebrated there. I recognized that in order to be
my best self as a Black woman, and for my employees to

be their best selves in service to the work we do on behalf of marginalized communities, we all needed rest to continue our fight.

I was happy to discover that there is data-driven research supporting this approach as well. A 2016 survey conducted by the travel industry and Harvard University found that people who take more vacation time have less stress and more satisfaction and success at work and in their personal lives. At Loveland, we implemented what we call seasonal rests, which offer employees two weeks paid time away in both the summer and winter seasons to recharge and recalibrate.

The fact remains that the same voice we use to advocate for justice is the one we must use to advocate for self-care. The same level of energy we harness to fight white supremacy should also be directed toward our mental, emotional, and physical restoration. The forward movement we want to make in the world and in our own lives must also allow us the space to rest, to recharge, to dream, and to reimagine.

WHAT DO WORK AND REST LOOK LIKE NOW?

IN OUR COLLECTIVE STRUGGLE TOWARD FREEDOM, WE all have a role to play. There are those who are focused on educating and those who run programs for the kids in schools. There are those practicing academic work and those focused on our physical healing. There are those doing organizing work within policy and those offering social services to our elders.

I hope, over my lifetime, to find a million ways to be a part of the work toward freedom. Whether I'm marching in the streets, making art, organizing, writing, opening my home to people who require rest and time for contemplation, or just having conversations steeped in kindness and intention—it all counts as "the work." It will look different at different times, and sometimes that difference won't sit right with people, as the only way some people know how to see "the work" is via struggle and martyrdom. I reject that notion. If the only way to do the work of an activist were truly through physical activism, such as marching and putting our bodies in harm's way, then only able-bodied people, people wealthy enough to take off work, or those with access to where the action is would be able to do it. And that is simply not the case.

I believe there is deep value in diversifying the ways we show up. I believe we can be activists in many different incarnations. And I believe we can press Pause when we need to rest. I'm looking forward to evolving as a learner, as a scholar, and as a speaker; to finding more effective, efficient ways to get my message out into the world. There is no deficit in the movement if I decide not to show up the same way I did in previous years. Also, I believe in the tag team nature of this work: While I am resting and not on the front lines of the fight, others will take the baton and run with it. And when I feel ready and rested, I will show up in all the ways I can for those who are ready to take their rest.

MY RESTED SELF IS
MY BEST SELF

I OFTEN SAY THAT MY HIGHEST SERVICE IS MY BEST SELF. When I am well rested, well nourished, and clearheaded, I am able to serve in the best way I can.

These days, as I write these words, I find my rest in following my own rhythms, seeking to step away from the rhythms of capitalism. I don't feel I have to be working all the time, and I understand that seasonal rest, time off, is restorative, not wasteful. I'm not following the rhythms of the patriarchy. I don't have a "biological clock" or a traditional time line that prioritizes getting married and having children before age forty. And with regard to my notions of success, I'm not following the rhythms of white supremacy or the belief that I must "keep up with the Joneses." I can find the joy in success that is defined by simplicity and ease, instead of hustle and grind.

Today, I reside with the motto "This, too, is 'the living.'" I insist that the most valuable parts of my life aren't only those that are productive or interesting under others' gaze. The living is also in the quiet moments of making myself a cup of tea, or sitting still and watching the river flow, or lying in a puddle of sunlight at home reading a book. These, too, are wildly worthy ways to spend our time and energy.

I also honor my natural rhythms. Paying attention to my needs depending on the time of day, the month, the year. I recognize that, in winter, I tend to dip into seasonal depression, so I try to keep my schedule light. I know that I have the most energy in the morning, so I try to serve myself by scheduling all my meetings before eleven. I also allow my highest values (ease, abundance, and opportunity) to guide me toward more ease and rest.

I give myself the space to be as expansive as I would like to be. I can be an activist and an academic; an artist, writer, and philanthropist; and someone who poses nude on her Instagram. My rest is in the freedom I demand of and offer myself. While a "harder, faster, stronger" lifestyle is one I previously celebrated, I now lean into the softer, slower, simpler version of being. I now have a chance to *experience* life, not just survive it.

It is yet another reimagined self.

ROAD MAP TO YOUR RENAISSANCE: REIMAGINING REST

LIVING IN CAPITALIST SOCIETIES, IT IS ALMOST IMPOS-sible to feel deserving of rest; thus, it is a concept that requires reimagining. First you must unlearn any beliefs that suggest that rest must be earned or, worse, that requiring rest is shameful. Rest is restorative, productive, and necessary. Rest is also pleasurable, indulgent, and fun. And you deserve it.

Consider how you can incorporate rest and ease into your own life and that of others. Remember: Your rested self is your best self.

ACTIVATE SELF-EMPATHY AND EMBRACE REST AS A BIRTHRIGHT. You are *deserving* of a comfortable, easeful, optimistic existence. Shift your mindset from the false belief that you must earn rest to the intrinsic knowledge that you *deserve* R&R and nourishment.

PRIORITIZE YOUR DREAM LIFE, YOUR REIMAGININGS. Determine what feeds your fantasies and soothes your nerves and then carve out regular time to tend to your body and soul. Consider what type of support—mental health therapy, spiritual mentoring, more time spent in nature, communing with friends—will offer you the most relief and ease.

INVEST IN COMMUNITY CARE. There are many organizations dedicated to offering rest to the most underserved communities. In an act of solidarity for our collective care consider paying your privilege forward.

MAPPING YOUR
OWN MANIFESTO

• •

Rest is a right I hold as a human being. Knowing that my best self is my highest service, I tend
generously to my rest and healing—mind, body,
and soul. I give myself permission to **let go of
perfectionism and invest energy into simply
being inspired by "the living."**

What do you need to give yourself permission
to do in order to allow yourself to rest? Add your
thoughts in place of the boldface text to define rest
in your own manifesto.

FINAL THOUGHTS

...

IT WAS NEARLY TEN YEARS AGO THAT I THOUGHT UP THE title for this book, around 2014. I was newly divorced, finally living in a big city, Washington, D.C., and I was inspired by the opportunity to reinvent myself. On the verge of a renaissance of my own, I remember the excitement of reimagining my future.

I have a small, yellow lined notebook in which I wrote in the middle of one of the pages, "A Renaissance of My Own." I liked how it looked on paper, a proper title for a book that had yet to be written. That same day, I went onto my social media pages and shared that it would be the title of a book I would one day write. I was putting out into the world my dream of being able to write the story of this big, bold reimagining that hadn't even unfolded yet. But I was certain it would happen, and I was confident that the glory of it would be worthy of publication. What I didn't know at the time was that, over the years, I would build an incredible community of readers and that, alongside them, I would grow, dream, and step into a renaissance of *our* making.

And here we are, in a time when reimagining the world is not just ideal but critical for our continued healing. Here we are, in a time when our goodness, our wellness, our livelihoods, are begging us to dream up bigger and bolder realities for ourselves and one another. Here we are, together, moving toward a renaissance that could very well reshape the world.

THE CHOSEN SELF

I WANT YOU TO REMEMBER THAT THIS JOURNEY ISN'T ONE of "finding" ourselves but, rather, of deciding who we want to be and boldly living out that truth. We often get caught up in the idea that we might be "missing the boat" with regard to our purpose, or our truest love, or our best self. I happen to believe that the only thing we're *supposed* to be doing is the thing that keeps us well, that makes us feel whole. It's the thing that, at the end of the day, allows us to feel we have lived a life that is true to us.

I recently read an article in which the author had replaced the language of one's "best self" with the language of one's "*chosen* self." That really shifted something in me. It reminded me that the hierarchy of "good, better, best" doesn't actually have a home in the conversation of our personal evolutions. Who you continue to be in the world should be aligned with ideas of nourishment and intention, rather than striving and struggling in an effort to be "the best."

MAYBE YOU *CAN* MANIFEST IT

THE ENTIRE WORLD IS COMPOSED OF MANIFESTED IDEAS that came from the minds of everyday people—people just like you, just like me; people who said, "I think *this* should be a reality." Everything, from our government to our educational curriculum, our ideas of family to our framework for love—each of these ideas came from minds that look just like yours. So, what does that tell you? It means that your mind can be used to shape reality, too.

I don't mean to make this sound easy—because it's not. It takes effort and commitment, especially when merely following the status quo is so simple to do. So, I'd like, for a moment, to harp on the difference between something that is *easy* and something that is *easeful*.

Easy can be defined as causing or involving little hardship or difficulty. *Easeful*—the type of ease I refer to with one of my highest values—refers to a state of comfort or peace. That peace is what comes from living in alignment with what matters most to us. It is what surfaces when we feel our hard work and efforts in life are actually going toward the things we value. That comfort is most tangible when we can exhale and rest well, knowing that we chose a life that feels good to us instead of one that just looks good to others.

I hope that the tools and inspiration in this book will guide you as you continue into the renaissance that is yours to claim. With your highest values, your own clear personal manifesto, and a willingness to see the world differently, you will have everything you need to stand firm in your truth and your power.

I look forward to witnessing the ways we continue to show up outside what the power structure and traditional frameworks have deemed as "right" or "best." No one knows what's better for us than we do. No one has the ability to chart our paths more carefully than we do. And no one can take away our fervor for a life we know is truly ours. Now is the time for us to start walking toward that renaissance—a renaissance of our own.

CREATE YOUR
OWN MANIFESTO

...

Use this space to combine the paragraphs of the manifesto you've altered to match your unique truth—thus creating a manifesto of your own.

ACKNOWLEDGMENTS

...

I HAVE SUCH OVERWHELMING GRATITUDE FOR MY COM- munity of readers—those who continue to learn and grow alongside me both online and in person. You have been an incredible source of inspiration, affirmation, and encourage- ment through the years and the milestones of both my life and my career. I feel so lucky to have you all in my world. I hope this book might be a nourishing part of our community.

To my team at Loveland. To The Loveland Group, LLC— Jules, Sula, Joe, Georgia, Rachel K., Channler, Therese, Monet, September, Phong, Serenity, Sonia, Julia, and our extended team, past and present, who each shined in their own lane of genius to support this project with grace, generosity, and shared expectation for what it could do in the world. And to the incredible team leading the efforts at The Loveland Foundation—Sharlene, Hannah, Miriam, TK, Chrystal, and Nikki—your diligence in our shared mission is a blessing to my heart and to the world. I can't thank you enough for con- tinuing to cultivate healing for so many, year after year.

Thank you to Tula and Lori, who held my story with such gentle hands, helping me to unfold my memories, make space for my feelings, honor my truth, and celebrate all that has been (and that could be). You both have been a deep warmth and joy in this process; I couldn't have done it without you.

To my agent, Rebecca, and editors, Chelcee and Marianne, thank you for believing in my story and my voice enough to shepherd me through to this opportunity to share it.

To my friends, family, and lovers, thank you for your patience, grace, and shared excitement as I labored through birthing this first book of mine; for offering me a soft place to land with my frustrations; for shining a light of possibility when I couldn't see it myself; for your suggestions and affirmations that helped shape the landscape of this book; and for your ongoing eagerness to celebrate this really special moment with me.

I'd also like to thank my intellectual and literary elders and ancestors who tilled the ground for the blooming gardens of my generation. I specifically would like to honor the work and influence of Nikki Giovanni, Angelina Weld Grimke, Toni Morrison, Alice Walker, Maya Angelou, James Baldwin, Angela Davis, Ana Julia Cooper, and countless others both past and present.

And to my mother for cultivating in me a love of reading, a respect for storytelling, and a belief that my voice deserved to be heard.

NOTES

...

INTRODUCTION

5 **in homage to the iconic photo:** Gloria Steinem and Dorothy Pitman Hughes, Dan Wynn Archive, 1971, National Portrait Gallery, Smithsonian Institution, npg.si.edu/object/npg_NPG .2005.121.

REFLECTIONS

53 **It was world-renowned psychologist:** Angela Duckworth, *Grit: The Power of Passion and Perseverance* (New York: Scribner, 2016), xx.

CHAPTER 2

74 **a podcast featuring Mia Birdsong:** Mia Birdsong, *How We Show Up: Reclaiming Family, Friendship, and Community* (New York: Hachette Go, 2020).

77 **A study put out in 2018:** Lisa I. Iezzoni et al., "Views of Teenage Children About the Effects of a Parent's Mobility Disability," *Disability Health Journal* 11, no. 3 (July 2018).

79 **In 2018, according to the U.S. Census:** U.S. Census Bureau, *Fertility of Women in the United States: 2018,* Table 2: "Children Ever Born, Number of Mothers, and Percent Childless by Age and

Marital Status, and by Nativity," June 2018, www.census.gov /data/tables/2018/demo/fertility/women-fertility.html#par _list_58.

80 **the highest percentage since 1976:** Amy Blackstone, *Childfree by Choice: The Movement Redefining Family and Creating a New Age of Independence* (New York: Dutton, 2019), xvii, 32.

80 **According to the Pew Research Center:** "Growing Share of Childless Adults in U.S. Don't Expect to Ever Have Children," Pew Research Center, November 2021, www.pewresearch.org/fact -tank/2021/11/19/growing-share-of-childless-adults-in-u-s -dont-expect-to-ever-have-children/.

80 **almost one in five women at age forty-five:** Denis Campbell, "Record Numbers of Women Reach 30 Child-Free in England and Wales," *The Guardian*, January 27, 2022.

80 **Although, in the United States, white women:** U.S. Census Bureau, *Fertility of Women in the United States: 2018*, Table 3a: "Children Ever Born per 1,000 Women and Percent Childless by Age, Marital Status, and Race: June 2018," www.census.gov /data/tables/2018/demo/fertility/women-fertility.html#par _list_59.

81 **The "Auntie" part is an homage to the "othermother":** Patricia Hill Collins, *Black Feminist Thought: Knowledge, Consciousness, and the Politics of Empowerment* (New York: Routledge, 2000), 178– 82, 189, 192, 193, 210.

81 **Collins writes that community othermothering:** Ibid., 192–93.

82 **And as sociologist Andrea S. Boyles:** Andrea S. Boyles, *You Can't Stop the Revolution: Community Disorder and Social Ties in Post-Ferguson America* (Oakland: University of California Press, 2019).

82 **twenty-first-century othermothers:** Andrea S. Boyles, "Following Harriet: A Note on Black Women and 'the Bringing' of the Black Community," October 30, 2019, drandreasboyles.com /public-commentary/f/following-harriet-tubman.

CHAPTER 3

90   **I read about the milestone suffrage marches:** National Women's
     History Museum, "Feminism: The First Wave," Women's His-
     tory, April 5, 2021, www.womenshistory.org/exhibits/feminism
     -first-wave-0.

90   **during the second wave of feminism:** National Women's History
     Museum, "Feminism: The Second Wave," Women's History,
     June 18, 2020, www.womenshistory.org/exhibits/feminism-sec
     ond-wave.

91   **conflated the Girlboss movement:** Amanda Mull, "The Girlboss
     Has Left the Building," *The Atlantic,* June 25, 2020.

95   **I had seen and adored the iconic 1970s photograph:** Wynn, 1970
     photo of Steinem and Pitman Hughes.

95   **Even with nearly five hundred thousand people:** Tim Wallace and
     Alicia Parlapiano, "Crowd Scientists Say Women's March in
     Washington Had 3 Times as Many People as Trump's Inaugu-
     ration," *The New York Times,* January 22, 2017, www.nytimes
     .com/interactive/2017/01/22/us/politics/womens-march-trump
     -crowd-estimates.html.

100 **In response to being asked to support the Fifteenth Amendment:**
     The House Joint Resolution Proposing the 15th Amendment to
     the Constitution, December 7, 1868, Enrolled Acts and Resolu-
     tions of Congress, 1789–1999, General Records of the United
     States Government, Record Group 11, National Archives and
     Records Administration, Washington, D.C.; see also "15th
     Amendment to the Constitution: Voting Rights (1870)," Mile-
     stone Documents, Archives.gov, www.archives.gov/milestone
     -documents/15th-amendment.

100 **Susan B. Anthony said:** Angela Y. Davis, *Women, Race and Class*
     (New York: Vintage Books, 1983), chap. 4; see also Sarah Gor-
     don, "White Supremacy and the Suffrage Movement," New
     -York Historical Society Museum and Library, April 2020,
     www.nyhistory.org/blogs/white-supremacy-and-the-suffrage
     -movement.

100 **While campaigning for women's right to vote:** Davis, *Women Race and Class*, chap. 4.

100 **Carrie Chapman Catt, who in 1920 founded:** Debra Michaels, "Carrie Chapman Catt," National Women's History Museum, 2015, www.womenshistory.org/education-resources/biographies /carrie-chapman-catt.

100 **"White supremacy shall be strengthened":** Chris Carsons and Virginia Kase, "Facing Hard Truths About the League's Origin," League of Women Voters, August 8, 2018, www.lwv.org/blog /facing-hard-truths-about-leagues-origin.

104 **It was then that I learned about women like Ida B. Wells:** Tianna Mobley, "Ida B. Wells-Barnett: Anti-Lynching and the White House," The White House Historical Association, April 2021, www.whitehousehistory.org/ida-b-wells-barnett-anti-lynching -and-the-white-house.

104 **I also read about Frances Ellen Watkins Harper:** Kerri Lee Alexander, "Frances Ellen Watkins Harper, (1825–1911)," National Women's History Museum, n.d., www.womenshistory .org/education-resources/biographies/frances-ellen-watkins -harper.

104 **Her speech, "We Are All Bound Up Together":** "(1866) Frances Ellen Watkins Harper, 'We Are All Bound Up Together,'" BlackPast, November 7, 2011, www.blackpast.org/african -american-history/speeches-african-american-history/1866 -frances-ellen-watkins-harper-we-are-all-bound-together/. See also Frances Ellen Watkins Harper, "We Are All Bound Up Together—May 1866," Carrie Chapman Catt Center for Women and Politics, Archives of Women's Political Communication, Iowa State University, awpc.cattcenter.iastate .edu/2017/03/21/we-are-all-bound-up-together-may-1866/.

105 **I struck gold one morning:** Bert J. Lowenberg and Ruth Bogin, eds., *Black Women in Nineteenth-Century American Life: Their Words, Their Thoughts, Their Feelings* (University Park, Pa.: Penn State University Press, 1976).

106 **Born into slavery in 1858:** Tyina Steptoe, "Anna Julia Haywood Cooper (1858–1964)," BlackPast, January 29, 2007, www.black past.org/african-american-history/cooper-anna-julia-hay wood-1858-1964/.

106 **Launched during the 1960s and '70s:** National Women's History Museum, "Feminism: The Second Wave."

106 **The second wave was ignited by Betty Friedan's:** Jacob Muñoz, "The Powerful, Complicated Legacy of Betty Friedan's 'The Feminine Mystique,'" *Smithsonian,* February 2021; Betty Friedan, *The Feminine Mystique* (New York: W. W. Norton, 1963).

106 **In it, Friedan rails against:** Debra Michals, ed., "Betty Friedan (1921–2006)," 2017, National Women's History Museum, www .womenshistory.org/education-resources/biographies/betty -friedan.

106 **The book hit a nerve with:** Robert McCrum, "The 100 Best Non-fiction Books: No. 18—*The Feminine Mystique* by Betty Friedan (1963)," *The Guardian,* May 30, 2016.

106 **The Black feminist theorist:** bell hooks, *Feminist Theory: From Margin to Center* (New York: Routledge, 1984), 1–2; see also Ashley Fetters, "4 Big Problems with 'The Feminine Mystique,'" *The Atlantic,* February 12, 2013.

107 **The second wave's focus on equal pay:** National Women's History Museum, "Feminism: The Second Wave."

107 **such as the forced sterilization:** Alexandra Minna Stern, "Forced Sterilization Policies in the US Targeted Minorities and Those with Disabilities—and Lasted into the 21st Century," *The Conversation,* in partnership with University of Michigan, August 26, 2020, ihpi.umich.edu/news/forced-sterilization-policies -us-targeted-minorities-and-those-disabilities-and-lasted-21st.

107 **into the 1970s, was legal:** Lutz Kaelber, "Eugenics: Compulsory Sterilization in 50 American States," Presentation at the 2012 Social Science History Association, University of Vermont, 2012, www.uvm.edu/~lkaelber/eugenics/.

107 **Even today, we see forced sterilization:** Minna Stern, "Forced Sterilization Policies"; see also Rachel Treisman, "Whistle-blower Alleges 'Medical Neglect,' Questionable Hysterectomies of ICE Detainees," NPR, September 16, 2020.

108 **Dr. Brittney Cooper's incredible book:** Brittney C. Cooper, *Beyond Respectability: The Intellectual Thought of Race Women* (Urbana: University of Illinois Press, 2017).

108 *Black Feminist Thought*: Patricia Hill Collins, *Black Feminist Thought: Knowledge, Consciousness and the Politics of Empowerment* (New York: Routledge, 2000).

108 **activists like Kimberlé Crenshaw:** Kory Stamper, "A Brief, Convoluted History of the Word 'Intersectionality,'" *The Cut*, March 9, 2018.

109 **coined the term** *intersectionality*: "Kimberlé Crenshaw's Intersectional Feminism," JSTOR Daily, August 1, 2020, daily.jstor.org /kimberle-crenshaws-intersectional-feminism/.

109 **Taking my cue from the wisewomen:** Keeanga-Yamahtta Taylor, "Until Black Women Are Free, None of Us Will Be Free," *The New Yorker*, July 20, 2020.

116 **fewer than twelve Black undergraduates each year:** Dennis O. Ojogho, "Affirmative Reaction: I, Too, Am Harvard," *The Harvard Crimson*, March 13, 2014, www.thecrimson.com/article /2014/3/13/ojogho-harvard-affirmative-action/.

120 **From time to time, I'll post a truth:** See Corinna Rosella's "White Privilege" stories on Instagram at @riseupgoodwitch.

122 **There's a line in the Langston Hughes poem:** Langston Hughes, "Freedom," *The Collected Works of Langston Hughes, Volume 1: The Poems: 1921–1940* (Columbia: University of Missouri Press, 2001).

CHAPTER 4

130 **I was thrilled to discover that Zora Neale Hurston:** "Zora Neale Hurston," Columbians Ahead of Their Time, Columbia 250, n.d., c250.columbia.edu/c250_celebrates/remarkable_columbians /zora_hurston.html.

131 **Toni Morrison was quoted:** Toni Morrison in conversation with Richard O. Moore, August 21, 2019, video and transcript, All Arts Vault Selects, WNET Group, www.allarts.org/programs /all-arts-vault-selects/the-all-arts-vault-toni-morrison-cpc9ku/.

133 **material spanning four thousand years of thought:** "About Columbia University Libraries," Columbia University Libraries, 2021, library.columbia.edu/about.html.

133 **All the Ivy League libraries are connected:** "BorrowDirect Resource Sharing Service," Ivy Plus Libraries Confederation, 2022, ivpluslibraries.org/programs/borrowdirect-resource-sharing -service/.

134 **public university tuition is free:** Lisa Goetz, "6 European Countries with Free College Tuition," Investopedia, June 18, 2022, www.investopedia.com/articles/personal-finance/080616/6 -countries-virtually-free-college-tuition.asp.

137 **"This campus still lives in the glory of 1893":** "The History of Columbia University," Columbia University in the City of New York, www.columbia.edu/content/history-columbia-university.

137 **a Black person wouldn't have been allowed:** Paulina Fcin, "The Treatment and Framing of Early Black Students at Columbia University," Columbia University & Slavery, Columbia University in the City of New York.

137 **And when we were finally allowed to matriculate:** "Post-1865: Students," Columbia University & Slavery, Columbia University in the City of New York.

137 **There had been an actual cross burning:** Thomas Germain, "'Bright Spots Giving Sign in a Dark Sky'—The Columbia University Cross Burning of 1924," Columbia University & Slavery, Columbia University in the City of New York.

138 **Critical Approaches in Social and Cultural Theory:** Columbia Institute for the Study of Sexuality and Gender, Critical Approaches in Social and Cultural Theory, Current Courses, Fall 2022.

138 **Gender and Sexuality in Africa:** Columbia University/London

School of Economics, Gender and Sexuality in Africa, Courses, Fall 2018.

139 **affirmative action:** Cornell Law School, Legal Information Institute, Wex, "affirmative action"; Merriam-Webster.com, Definition of "affirmative action."

139 **according to many studies,** *white women:* Sally Kohn, "Affirmative Action Has Helped White Women More than Anyone," *Time,* June 17, 2013; Tim Wise, "Is Sisterhood Conditional?," *National Women's Studies Journal* 10, no. 3 (Autumn 1998).

141 **On April 11, 2019, Alexander McNab:** Sharon Otterman, "Black Columbia Student's Confrontation with Security Becomes Flashpoint over Racism on Campus," *The New York Times,* April 18, 2019.

142 **He declined to show it:** Alexander McNab, "I Am More than My ID," The Eye, *Columbia Spectator,* April 23, 2019, columbia spectator.com/the-eye/2019/04/23/i-am-more-than-my-id/.

142 **But several other students filmed the incident:** Otterman, "Black Columbia Student's Confrontation with Security."

142 **reminiscent of the thousands of public lynchings:** NAACP, "History of Lynching in America," naacp.org/find-resources /history-explained/history-lynching-america.

143 **Some spectators even held picnics:** Equal Justice Initiative, *Lynching in America: Confronting the Legacy of Racial Terror,* 3rd ed., eji.org/reports/lynching-in-america/.

143 **where a paltry 5.2 percent of the student body:** Table: "Enrollment by Race and Ethnicity, Columbia University in the City of New York," Data USA, n.d., datausa.io/profile/university/columbia -university-in-the-city-of-new-york#enrollment_race.

143 **By the Monday after the incident:** For a link to the petition, see GWC-UAW Local 2110, "Statement on Barnard Public Safety," ColumbiaGradUnion, columbiagradunion.org/2019/04/24/state ment-on-barnard-public-safety/; Otterman, "Black Columbia Student's Confrontation with Security."

144 **Later that day, the Columbia undergraduate deans:** Mary C. Boyce,

Lisa Rosen-Metsch, and James J. Valentini, "Addressing Racism on Our Campus," News and Updates, Columbia College, Columbia University, April 2019, www.college.columbia.edu /news/addressing-racism-our-campus; Elina Arbo, "Responding to Racism: Analyzing Columbia and Barnard's Messages Around Five Anti-Black Incidents on Campus," *Columbia Spectator*, April 17, 2019.

144 **The president of Barnard:** "Statement on the Recent Campus Incident," News, Barnard College, Columbia University, April 12, 2019, barnard.edu/news/statement-recent-campus-incident.

144 **Ultimately, five officers and their supervisors:** Valeria Escobar, "Barnard Public Safety Officers Put on Administrative Leave Following Physical Confrontation of Black Student," *Columbia Spectator*, April 12, 2010.

146 **a low rate of tenured minority professors:** Office of the Provost, Columbia University, "Faculty Diversity," Slide 3: "Representation of Race and Ethnicity among Full-Time Faculty by School/ Division and Faculty Status," n.d., provost.columbia.edu /content/faculty-diversity.

149 **From Frederick Douglass to Malcolm X:** "On the Enormous Contributions of Black Autodidacts," Remembering History (blog), September 24, 2018, www.rememberinghistory.com/news /2018/9/24/on-the-enormous-contributions-of-black-auto didacts.

156 **a rise in the number of homeschoolers:** Carolyn Thompson, "As U.S. Schools Reopen, Many Families Continue to Opt for Homeschooling," *NewsHour*, PBS, April 14, 2022.

156 **are turning to homeschooling:** Casey Parks "The Rise of Black Homeschooling," *The New Yorker*, June 14, 2021.

CHAPTER 5

163 **her umbrella company, Harpo Productions:** Harpo Productions, LinkedIn, www.linkedin.com/company/harpo-productions/.

163 **produced the movies *Beloved*, *Precious*, and *Selma*:** "With Harpo

Films," IMDb, www.imdb.com/search/title/?companies=c0000
4231.

173 **after the murder of George Floyd:** Jason Silverstein, "The Global
Impact of George Floyd: How Black Lives Matter Protests
Shaped Movements Around the World," CBS News, June 4,
2021.

173 **by the name of Valerie Wade:** "Valerie Wade, M.A., C.A.," in
"Our Team of Storytellers," The Skinny House, skinnyhouse
.org/team.

175 **companies began waking up:** Geri Stengel, "Black Lives Matter
Protests Move Corporate D&I Initiatives Center Stage," *Forbes*,
June 17, 2020.

178 **Black teenagers were more likely to attempt suicide:** Meghan
Romanelli et al., "Factors Associated with Distinct Patterns
of Suicidal Thoughts, Suicide Plans, and Suicide Attempts
Among US Adolescents," *Prevention Science*, September 4, 2021,
pubmed.ncbi.nlm.nih.gov/34482517/; see also Christina Caron,
"Why Are More Black Kids Suicidal? A Search for Answers,"
The New York Times, November 18, 2021.

178 **Black people living below the poverty line:** Office of Minority
Health, "Mental and Behavioral Health—African Americans,"
U.S. Department of Health and Human Services, n.d., www
.minorityhealth.hhs.gov/omh/browse.aspx?lvl=4&lvlid=24.

182 **Matriarchal systems:** Harriet Marsden, "International Women's
Day: What Are Matriarchies, and Where Are They Now?," *The
Independent*, March 8, 2018; see also Dr. Heide Goettner-
Abendroth and Cécile Keller, "Matriarchy," International
Academy HAGIA for Modern Matriarchal Studies, n.d., www
.hagia.de/en/international-academy-hagia/.

183 **and when the market crashes:** Ben Carlson, "How Often Should
You Expect a Stock Market Correction?," A Wealth of Common
Sense, January 20, 2022, awealthofcommonsense.com/2022/01
/how-often-should-you-expect-a-stock-market-correction/.

183 **Of those who lost their jobs:** Kim Parker, Rachel Minkin, and Jesse Bennett, "Economic Fallout from Covid-19 Continues to Hit Lower-Income Americans the Hardest," Pew Research Center, September 24, 2020, www.pewresearch.org/social -trends/2020/09/24/economic-fallout-from-covid-19-con tinues-to-hit-lower-income-americans-the-hardest/.

183 **all the job losses were of those held by women:** Annalyn Kurtz, "The US Economy Lost 140,000 Jobs in December. All of Them Were Held by Women," CNN, January 8, 2021.

183 **most of those jobs had been held by women of color:** Diana Boesch and Shilpa Phadke, "When Women Lose All the Jobs: Essential Actions for a Gender-Equitable Recovery," Center for American Progress, February 1, 2021, www.americanprogress.org /article/women-lose-jobs-essential-actions-gender-equitable -recovery/.

CHAPTER 6

193 **I once read that Albert Einstein:** Joe Nally, "Joe Nally Journal: 'I Thought of That While Riding My Bicycle—Albert Einstein,'" Rider Journal, The British Continental, April 21, 2020, thebrit ishcontinental.co.uk/2020/04/21/joe-nally-journal-i-thought -of-that-while-riding-my-bicycle-albert-einstein/.

194 **The late, great writer Toni Morrison:** "12 of Toni Morrison's Most Memorable Quotes," *The New York Times,* August 6, 2019; see also "Toni Morrison at Portland State, May 30, 1975," PDF of transcript, www.mackenzian.com/wp-content/uploads/2014/07 /Transcript_PortlandState_TMorrison.pdf.

196 **The government also required that we share:** *The Code of Federal Regulations* (§1291.50: Monitoring of the General Fund and Targeted Funds, 2022), U.S. Department of Housing and Urban Development, www.ecfr.gov/current/title-12/chapter-XII/subchap ter-E/part-1291/subpart-E/section-1291.50.

197 **We have a lower life expectancy:** Latoya Hill, Samantha Artiga, and Sweta Haldar, "Key Facts on Health and Health Care by

Race and Ethnicity," KKF, January 26, 2022, www.kff.org/racial
-equity-and-health-policy/report/key-facts-on-health-and
-health-care-by-race-and-ethnicity/.

197 **In New York City, where I live:** New York State Department of
Health, *New York State Report on Pregnancy-Associated Deaths
in 2018* §4: "Finding from the 2018 Cohort," www.health.ny
.gov/community/adults/women/docs/maternal_mortality
_review_2018.pdf.

202 **Because, as Langston Hughes said:** Hughes, "Freedom."

204 *How to Do Nothing:* Jenny Odell, *How to Do Nothing: Resisting
the Attention Economy* (Brooklyn, N.Y.: Melville House, 2019).

210 **A 2016 survey conducted by the travel industry:** Shawn Achor and
Michelle Gielan, "The Data-Driven Case for Vacation," *Harvard Business Review,* July 13, 2016, hbr.org/2016/07/the-data
-driven-case-for-vacation.

RACHEL E. CARGLE is an Akron, Ohio–born public academic, writer, and lecturer working at the intersection of race and womanhood. She is the creator of The Great Unlearn, an online learning space that provides resources and critical discourse with a monthly curriculum taught by Black academics and thinkers whose work points the way toward a more equitable future. She is also the founder of Elizabeth's of Akron, a bookstore and writing center that promotes, amplifies, and celebrates marginalized voices. She founded The Loveland Foundation, which, through its Therapy Fund for Black Women and Girls, offers free mental health care.

rachelcargle.com

Instagram: rachel.cargle

Twitter: RachelCargle

facebook.com/rachelecargle